PLAIN

LANGUAGE

PLEADINGS

Carol Ann Wilson

Litigation Forms in Plain Language
with
Arguments for Plain Language
in
Legal Documents

Prentice Hall
Upper Saddle River, New Jersey 07458

Library of Congress Cataloging-in-Publication Data
Wilson, Carol Ann, [date].
   Plain language pleadings / Carol Ann Wilson.
     p. cm.
   "Litigation forms in plain language with arguments for plain
language in legal documents."
   Includes bibliographical references and index.
   ISBN 0-13-199639-8 (alk. paper)
    1. Legal composition. 2. Law—United States—Language. 3. Legal
documents—United States. 4. Pleading—United States. I. Title.
KF250.W55   1996
808'.06634—dc20   95-45390
                                           CIP

Copyright © 1996 by Carol Ann Wilson
Published by PRENTICE HALL, INC., Upper Saddle River, NJ 07458

Printed in the United States of America
10 9 8 7 6 5 4 3 2 1

ISBN 0-13-199639-8

"This publication is designed to provide accurate and authoritative information
in regard to the subject matter covered. It is sold with the understanding that
the publisher is not engaged in rendring legal, accounting, or other professional
service. If legal advice or other expert assistance is required, the services of a
competent professional person should be sought."
*—From the Declaration of Principles jointly adopted by a Committee of the
American Bar Association and a Committee of Publishers and Associations*

Permissions to reprint:
David Mellinkoff, reprinted from *Legal Writing, Sense and Nonsense*, ©1982, with permission of the
West Publishing Company; Mark McCormack, *The Terrible Truth About Lawyers* (©1988), reprinted
by permission of Mark Reiter, Executive Editor; Bryan Garner, *The Elements of Legal Style* (©1991),
reprinted by permission of Oxford University Press; Joseph Kimble, *Plain English: A Charter for
Clear Writing* (©1992), reprinted by permission of Thomas M. Cooley Law Review; The Decline and
Fall of Gobbledygook: A Report on Plain Language Documentation (©1990), reprinted by permission
of the Canadian Bar Association and the Canadian Bankers' Association; David C. Elliott, "A Model
Plain-Language Act," reprinted with permission of the *Texas Bar Journal*, December 1993, Volume
56, page 1,118; Noelle C. Nelson, reprinted from *A Winning Case* (©1991) with permission of
Prentice-Hall, Inc.; John M. O'Quinn, reprinted from "The Art of Jury Selection; Plaintiff's
Techniques," (©1994), by permission of John M. O'Quinn; and United States District Judge Lynn
Hughes, reprinting from his local rules and seminar materials by permission.

Prentice-Hall International (UK) Limited,London
Prentice-Hall of Australia Pty. Limited, Sydney
Prentice-Hall Canada Inc., Toronto
Prentice-Hall Hispanoamericana, S.A., Mexico
Prentice-Hall of India Private Limited, New Delhi
Prentice-Hall of Japan, Inc., Tokyo
Pearson Education Asia Pte. Ltd., Singapore
Editora Prentice-Hall do Brasil, Ltda., Rio de Janeiro

DEDICATION

A Funeral for Legalese

"I must admit, it hurts to see them go," she cried,
As tears welled up and she ached inside.
"The wherefores and the witnesseths,
 The and/ors, saids, and saiths;
 All must be taken for their last ride."

"But maybe not yet, as we can sprinkle a few,
 Here and there, as morning meets the dew."
They were such good friends to her, and
She tolerated their useless cry and hue.
To no longer have them made her somewhat blue.

"But progress is upon us, and we must communicate."
She thought about the words she had lately grown to hate,
Like "comes now," "subscribed," and "cause."
"Oh, if I keep this up, I surely will be late."

She wouldn't miss the funeral,
She danced and sang with glee,
For legalese was passing away,
It never more would be.

"Ring the bells and sound the gong!"
 She screamed from atop her desk;
"They've already been around much too long;
 They MUST be laid to rest."

Carol Ann Wilson

CONTENTS

Contents

FOREWORD

Read this book.

The first four chapters will tell you why.
The last four chapters will tell you how to write.

If the name *Cool Hand Luke* were available, it would
be appropriate for one of these chapters. In that movie,
Paul Newman's character is told:

"What we have here is a failure to communicate."

We lawyers frequently have that problem, too.

This book, written by the best lawyer's assistant I have
ever had the pleasure of knowing, can help to correct
that problem.

I hope she writes a sequel, and I hope it's
"How to Take a Short Deposition."

Joe H. Reynolds
Attorney at Law

PREFACE

I love and respect the law, and I love and respect lawyers. Lawyers are interesting, intriguing people. Good lawyers work miracles. I have witnessed some of those miracles in the courtroom, in depositions, mediations, settlement negotiations, and in many hours of selfless, pro bono work. Lawyers rule our world. Most of our legislators, chief executives, statesmen, and world leaders have been lawyers or trained in the law. Successful lawyering requires an excellent mind, but also an excellent staff.

I have spent 25 years working with lawyers, helping lawyers, and teaching legal secretaries and legal assistants. Lawyers, as professionals, should employ professionals to staff their offices. The lawyer's image needs to be improved. The professional lawyer's assistant (LA) can help with that improvement by being professional and by caring as much about the law and the legal system as the lawyer. The conduct and the work product of the LA reflect on the lawyer-employer.

Lawyers'poor writing skills contribute to clients' and the general public's disdain for lawyers and ultimately to lawyer-bashing. Scattering legalese throughout a document compounds poor writing. Poorly written documents that grow into form files perpetuate more bad writing, and bad writing impedes communication. We must communicate before we can win.

In working with lawyers in three states, I have had valuable opportunities to learn; those lawyers have been patient enough to teach me. I have studied ethics, served as a lay member of a state bar grievance committee, and even served on a grand jury. I know what I can and cannot do as a nonlawyer. I know what will get lawyers in trouble and what will keep them out of trouble.

Through these rewarding years of assisting lawyers, I have been given many responsibilities, including drafting pleadings, briefs, and other legal documents (always, of course, under the supervision of a lawyer). Sometimes even a skeleton draft was just that needed "push" to get the lawyer started on a writing project.

LAs should realize the value of good writing to the lawyer and improve their own writing skills. LAs who understand legal writing can also help to improve it.

The legal profession is wallowing in a world of worthless words. Lawyers must write concisely and must begin by eliminating legalese. They must organize their documents. They must follow the rules. They must *communicate*. Their communication must be powerful and persuasive.

"Jesus wept." The shortest sentence in the Bible. Two words. Two powerful words. Those two words stir emotions. Legal writers must become aware of the *power* of conciseness. When groping through long, muddled phrases and paragraphs, we might remember the power of this sentence.

We also might remember its conciseness. Some lawyers might have written: "Clad in a heavy robe which paralleled the heaviness he felt in his heart, and lumbering under the weight of the sins of all the ages, Jesus, the son of Mary and Joseph, whose remaining days were fewer than any of his disciples realized, succumbed to the sentiments, pressures, and mental anguish of those recent days which would leave their mark on history for all time, and, unable to stem the flood of salty tears whose force would insist upon being unleashed, cried as He had never cried before and never would again."

By the time we reach the end of this sentence, we have forgotten where we started or what we were trying to accomplish. This is exactly what has happened to much of our legal writing, which *should be* powerful and persuasive. Instead it is gibberish, frustrating, and forgettable.

That's not to say that we can't tell a good story or include pertinent details in our legal writing. Instead, we need to do some better thinking and planning as we outline our writing projects.

I hope this book will inspire lawyers' assistants to improve their skills and earn respect for their abilities. I hope some of that inspiration will transfer to their lawyers. I hope that lawyers will encourage their LAs to increase their knowledge and have confidence in their abilities.

We have gotten into this serious trouble because we rely on forms rather than on thinking. If our pleadings have ended with "Wherefore Premises Considered" for 40 years, how can we take it out? Rather than ask, "Does this serve any purpose?," we yield to mindless custom.

Concise writing takes organizational skills. It takes clear thinking to write a plain language document. It must be *reader-directed*. That's one key ingredient missing from our pleadings. Our reader is the judge, opposing counsel, the client, and the appellate panel. If our documents communicate, if they are easily understood, they will satisfy every reader.

Unfortunately, lawyers don't write reader-friendly documents. They write as if they are anticipating an argument, and they weaken their points by throwing in phrases to ward off argument. Judges are tired of wading through legalese to find a point. How do we get the judge's attention? The answer is simple: we don't, if we continue to write that way.

The LA with clear thinking and writing skills is invaluable to the lawyer. The lawyer can devote time to the intricacies of the law, while the LA can make sure that the document makes sense and communicates with the reader. We will then have good documents that keep our clients and our adversaries informed. Our work will be remembered. Our writing will help to win lawsuits.

If we improve our writing, our thinking, and our product, we will:

- Improve the legal team

- Impress the client

- Improve the lawyer's image

- Increase the lawyer's business

- Improve the legal system

Every competent LA can put this book to good use. The *really* competent ones will get their lawyers to read it.

The truly great legal teams—lawyers and LAs—will integrate plain language into all their writing.

ACKNOWLEDGMENTS

To those great, forward-thinking leaders of the plain language movement for lawyers, I am indebted. You are cutting a widening path through legal gobbledygook. David Mellinkoff, Joseph Kimble, Bryan Garner, George Hathaway, David Elliott, Dr. Robert Eagleson of Sydney, Australia; the bar associations of Michigan, Texas, Missouri, Canada, and Australia; all the members of Clarity, including David P. Sellar in Scotland, Philip Knight of British Columbia, Sir Kenneth Keith of New Zealand, Michéle Asprey of New South Wales: you are my heroes. Thank you for bringing sense to legal writing.

To my mentors, who have taught and encouraged me as I have learned how to assist lawyers: Jim Diamond, Bob Holt, and Judge Joe C. Morris of Jackson, Tennessee; Ed Pyle and Claude Ramer of Nashville; Tom Hullverson, Jim Hullverson, John Frank, and Charles Abele of St. Louis; Joe Reynolds, Charles Peterson, George Bishop, Grant Cook, Judge Lamar McCorkle, and Judge Lynn Hughes of Houston—I owe you so much. My wish is that every LA could have such patient, caring teachers.

To my friends, lawyers, and educators who gave their time in reviewing drafts of this book—Kay Morgan, Suzanne Goss, Joe Reynolds, Mary Ann McCarty, Dr. Hugh Welch, and Devon Kirk—your input was vital and I feel fortunate to have had it.

And to all the LAs out there: Keep up your good work. Be patient and understanding with your lawyers and other legal team members, and always give them your best. Always look for ways to improve our product.

Carol Ann Wilson

CHAPTER 1

An Argument for
Plain Language

Where Are We and
How Did We Get Here?

Legal writing is a mess. It's wordy and not easily understood. Clients hate it. Judges hate it. It damages the lawyer's reputation almost as much as Rambo tactics. LAs (lawyers' assistants) must help.

We must communicate. We're not doing that very well. We should make our writing powerful. We must think succinctly. We must organize smoothly. We must use powerful words. We must pare the legalese, the useless formalisms, the mindless Latin words and phrases, and the otherwise utterly meaningless words from our writing. We must edit, edit, and edit again. Can we say it in three words instead of ten? In four instead of a paragraph? In two instead of four?

Why must we do it? To get the reader's attention, to persuade, to convince, to be remembered, to be effective in our arguments, and to save *time*. We can't make any more time—we can only make the most of that most precious commodity. The clients who keep law firms in business must be able to understand the writings for which they pay

1

handsomely. Judges must be impressed by, and interested in, what we have to say.

Today's emerging trend is toward "plain language" in legal documents. There is a worldwide Plain Language movement that is affecting the legal profession. Sophisticated clients are beginning to insist on it. They are withholding payment for needless hours spent by many lawyers working on one incomprehensible document.

Excessively lengthy documents have no place in today's fast-paced society. Most people don't have time to read them. A lawyer's clients don't have time to read them. Judges don't have time to read them. Appellate rules include length limits for briefs and require special permission from the court (rarely granted) to exceed those limits. In the past, those limits have been stated in pages. New rules being formulated as this book is written contain *word limits* (12,500 words for a federal appellant's brief). (That takes care of those who thought they were beating the system by using small type, narrow margins, and a multitude of footnotes.)

Both the federal rules and most state rules of civil procedure have limits for interrogatories. Proposed new federal rules severely limit *all* discovery. Limitations force writers to be concise and not waste words. Lawyers must plan their documents with more care. They must organize their thinking so that they can produce organized documents. Those who do not do so are often ineffective.

It was once said by a lawyer trying to defend a 75-page lease he had written: "At least with a stick of dynamite, you can be sure the fly is dead." We don't need a stick of dynamite. We need a laser-guided missile. We need precise, powerful writing.

Words are the weapons of litigation—too many words can create needless litigation; incorrect use of them breeds misunderstanding; and correct use of them wins lawsuits. A contract filled with long, hard-to-understand sentences can foster litigation to correct its meaning. But carefully chosen words settle disputes and win lawsuits. A well-written collection letter can avert a suit. A well-written fee agreement can eliminate disagreements with clients. A well-written complaint hastens, rather than delays, the litigation process. A well-written speech is remembered and sometimes quoted. A well-written letter is saved, treasured, and sometimes published. A well-written jury charge is *understood*.

To be well written, a document must convey the intended message and that message must be obvious. We should not have to dig and search and question the meaning of a document. If it's clearly written, there is no doubt as to its meaning. Nor should an adversary be justified in filing *another* document asking a judge to order us to explain what we meant. Yet how many times a day does that happen in lawsuits across America? Rule 12 should not be resorted to simply because our pleadings are not clear. But defense lawyers look for ways to file a Rule 12 motion, and that causes delays.

Killer Procrastination

Some lawyers need help with the craft of writing itself. Some need help in making sure they've written what they meant to say. Others need help in just getting started.

We make jokes about lawyers waiting till the last minute to do something. We say their best law school grades must have been in Procrastination 101. The trait is so prevalent, we can properly describe it as notorious. Why do lawyers become notorious procrastinators?

The reason lawyers seem to procrastinate is that they are forced to practice crisis management—especially the trial lawyers. Litigation sometimes requires flameproof suits and hard hats, because trial lawyers are constantly putting out fires and heading off deadline dizziness. They sometimes need help getting *started* on those projects that are not yet on fire, but are simmering on the back burner. That's where we LAs can give some of our best help.

Concise writing takes time. It's easy for a lawyer to say, "Get me that motion we filed in the Griffin case." Then we dutifully find it, substitute names and a few details, and crank out another motion filled with needless words just like Griffin and the hundreds before it. Bad writing regenerates itself and fosters more bad writing. Then it becomes acceptable due to the sheer number of repetitions! It's part of the "we've always done it that way" disease.

Procrastination is frequently at fault. We have not planned our time and must rush to get something done at the deadline. Then it's too late to think about our words and write the document in plain language.

Let's Get Rid of Limiting Labels

One million lawyers are expected to be practicing in the United States by the year 2000. Many will do their own writing; many will rely on assistants for some of that writing. I call that assistant the "lawyer's assistant," whether male or female, whether called a legal secretary, legal assistant, paralegal, or law clerk. Those terms are used and understood both interchangeably and with different meanings, depending on who's doing the talking, who's doing the listening, and who's doing the labeling. But limiting an individual because of labels is nearly always a mistake.

In a small law office, there may be one employee on staff, who serves as legal secretary, legal assistant, law clerk, courthouse runner, copy clerk, coffee maker, and cleaning person. That person is the LA. In large firms, secretaries may be forbidden from making copies or going to court. There may be severe lines of demarcation separating the legal secretary, the legal assistant, and the law clerk. Those differences depend upon firm policy, and firm policies differ widely.

For a team to function at its best, all team members, regardless of title, must respect each other and must respect each other's talents. All members must know the roles the others play. In many offices the duties of the legal secretary and the paralegal overlap. If feelings are hurt when one performs the other's duties, the effectiveness of the legal team is damaged. But if all team members know what the goals are, what the project entails, and what the lawyer needs, that team can work miracles.

The important point to know and remember is that *each* team member is the LA. The person who attends to the details of scheduling a deposition is the LA. The person who checks citations and quotations in a brief is the LA. The person who handles the phone is the LA, as that person shields the lawyer from interruptions or handles matters that might not require the lawyer's personal, immediate attention.

When we must get something filed by 5 p.m., the person making the copies at 4:30 is the most important person on the team. We can't get the pleading filed if we can't get it copied and out the door. And that copy clerk will function better in an emergency if treated with respect at all other times.

A common problem not discussed as often as it should be, is that of some paralegals' treating secretaries with disdain. This impairs the proper functioning of the legal services delivery team. There are ineffective staff members everywhere. A title does not make one important; *abilities* do. All LAs should improve their abilities at every opportunity and should never become complacent or think they have no more to learn.

Drafting Legal Documents

Of course, the person who drafts pleadings and documents for the lawyer is the LA. Law firms may give staff members certain labels; it is necessary to do so for purposes of organization. This book, however, is not meant to differentiate among the labels assigned to law office staff members. This is a reference work for anyone in the law office—including lawyers—who drafts documents.

The LA who can draft pleadings is valuable to the lawyer. Many times the lawyer functions best if something just gets *started*. I've known many lawyers who hate to get started on a pleading, even if a great form file is available. It's easy to put it off to the last minute. The LA who anticipates the lawyer's needs and gets something started is worth a lot to the lawyer. If that LA understands the power of plain language, that's ideal.

That LA is also valuable to the legal *profession* because the LA is in a position to help the lawyer get rid of legalese and legaldegook. The LA should understand a legal document, even if only to a small extent. If the competent LA cannot understand the meaning of a written document, especially a pleading, there is probably some way to improve it.

Clients Are Concerned

Clients, and the public in general, are becoming more sophisticated and knowledgeable. They now *want* to know what these documents mean. It's not enough any more to think that the lawyer knows what it means and so that's all right. It's not all right. It's not all right to assume the client *expects* it, either. That's a copout used by lawyers who are afraid to write simply.

If the client isn't happy, what happens? The bill isn't paid, or the client doesn't come back or send referral business. Lawyers cannot survive with such clients. There may not be enough of them to go around.

Let the client know what's going on. Keep him happy. Keep him as a client. To do that, the lawyer must communicate well with the client. Lawyers *must* use plain language in their pleadings and other documents to save precious time for everyone affected, as well as to improve their client relations and their image in general.

The widespread use of plain language documents should save countless hours every year for lawyers, their secretaries and legal assistants, opposing counsel and their staffs, and judicial personnel, including briefing clerks and staffs.

The word—both written and spoken—is the lifeblood of the lawyer. It must be improved. No one can afford the time wasted by miscommunication. No lawyer can afford to offend clients. *Without the client, we have no purpose.* Let's make the client proud of us and proud of our work. Let's have clients who refer others to our firms because we communicate well. Let's aspire to be respected as invaluable problem-solvers. Wouldn't it be wonderful to hear a client say, "Thank you for not talking over my head"?

The Trend Toward Plain Language

New York, California, Texas, and Florida are considered bellwethers of legal trends in substantive law. But it was the State Bar of Michigan that began the plain language movement in earnest. The forward thinkers in the Michigan Bar created a Plain English Committee. Texas and Missouri have joined the fight. (Since most of my experience has been in Texas, you will hear more about Texas in this book.) The movement's most notable pioneer was David Mellinkoff, now law professor emeritus at UCLA.

Resorting to a cliché, I must recognize Professor David Mellinkoff as the "grandaddy of them all." In 1963 he wrote *The Language of the Law*[1] which opened many eyes, but not all. He kept fighting. He kept writing. He knew the trend was there and that something had to be done because lawyers were failing to communicate. In 1982 he wrote *Legal Writing: Sense and Nonsense.*[2] After many law review articles and many years as a law school professor, he completed *Mellinkoff's Dictionary of American Legal Usage*[3] in 1992.

George Hathaway, Chair of the Michigan Bar's Plain English Committee, says that "[e]very lawyer, legal assistant, and legal secretary should have a copy on their desk and follow it. If they did, they wouldn't hear so many lawyer jokes."[4]

Mellinkoff has hope that "a new day is dawning" with the "profusion of incisive articles and books, bytes, and megabytes" that are fueling the plain English movement.[5]

Every year seminars are offered for lawyers—especially litigators—to teach them how to write more effectively and thus be more *persuasive.* Judges dislike "legaldegook" and "legalese" and are reflecting that dislike in their rulings and opinions. The word legalese really doesn't need to be in quotations marks any longer. Nearly everybody knows what it is—certainly everybody in the legal field.

Background

Too many attorneys these days do not yield to modern pleading practice. They try to turn back the clock to the dawn of the common law, when pleading was highly technical and any defect in pleading was fatal. Even today, lawyers continue to use their doublets and triplets to obscure every simple, concise thought and believe this to be necessary.

At English common law, pleadings were used to define the issues for trial. Issues were selected and narrowed by an exchange of pleadings and a series of exceptions and demurrers.[6] At common law, pleading was the only form of *discovery* available. Think about that for a moment while you appreciate the full effect of the state of things at that time. *Pleadings* were *discovery*. As we work with modern-day discovery practices, that's a difficult concept to understand, but that's the way it was. Pleadings were required to be so detailed as to address that huge area we know today as the discovery phase of a lawsuit.

In Texas, this form of "discovery" was adopted by the Republic of Texas in 1836.[7] Dust off some old opinions, especially the ones that quote portions of the pleadings, and you will be amazed. It was truly a forum for the beauty of the written word—but not very practical as our lives became more complicated.

Beginning of Change

In the 1920s, however, legal scholars began to advocate the theory that cases should be resolved based upon their *facts*—not upon technical rules of pleading. In order to promote full disclosure of the facts, it was proposed that pleadings be relegated to the function of *simply giving notice* of the type of claim involved. Today that's called "notice pleading."

The development of the facts and the narrowing of the issues was left to other devices, such as Interrogatories, Requests for Admission, Requests for Production, and Depositions, all of which we now refer to as the "discovery" phase of a lawsuit.

The Federal Rules of Civil Procedure, adopted in 1938, codified this integrated pretrial process to define and narrow the issues. Gone (or to be gone—once lawyers caught on) were pleadings which rivaled *War and Peace* for length. In their place was the huge area of *discovery*, so that by the time of trial, everybody knew what everybody else had, and where they stood, and what the lawsuit was probably worth. Settlements were then justified. Today maybe ten percent of all lawsuits actually go to trial.

The Purpose of Modern Pleadings

Under modern pleading practice, led by the federal rules, the purpose of pleadings is to *give notice*. Pleadings indicate, generally, the type of litigation; discovery refines the issues. Fact pleading is not only discouraged—it is prohibited. (Read Rule 8 of the Federal Rules of Civil Procedure. Some states may still require fact pleading, but they are bucking the trend as well as all good sense.) Don't misunderstand: your pleadings will contain facts. Many lawyers plan their trials around the allegations in the relevant pleading. That's as it should be—*if* the pleading is well written.

The notice pleading philosophy is clearly carried through in the Appendix of Forms attached to each year's revision of the Federal Rules of Civil Procedure. An examination of these forms shows that pleading is to be extremely basic—"plain vanilla," I submit. No detailed facts are pled. Notice is given to the defendant that the cause of action arises out of a motor vehicle accident, or a breach of contract, or a violation of antitrust statutes, or whatever, and that the defendant was negligent. To repeat: development of the detailed facts is left to discovery.

Plaintiff's pleading should say little more than "you hurt me and I am entitled to $_____ in damages." Defendant's pleading might say little more than "I didn't do it and I expect you to prove that I did" and might add "but if I did, it was somebody else's fault." Not in those words, but you get the idea. The basics.

States Follow the Lead

Since 1941, states have followed the United States Supreme Court's lead. Rules of civil procedure have been adopted by many states, establishing the same type of unified pretrial scheme for the definition and narrowing of issues as that incorporated in the federal rules.

Unfortunately, now more than 50 years later, some attorneys have not yet accepted this integrated process. They continue to waste valuable time by trying to preserve the ancient common law practice of discovery by pleadings through the use of wordy petitions and special exceptions before answer.

Appellate courts in Texas have done their best to educate and inform these recalcitrant attorneys. They have held that the sole purpose of pleading is to provide fair notice to the opponent.[8] Texas courts have defined fair notice as pleading with "sufficient specificity to allow an opposing attorney of *reasonable competence* to ascertain the nature of the basic issues in controversy."[9]

This, then, is the test to be applied by the trial courts in considering special exceptions: whether a defense attorney of reasonable competence can ascertain the nature of the basic issues in controversy. If your initial pleading does that, that is all that is required. Look at any of the forms in the Appendix of Forms in West Publishing Company's paperback *Federal Rules of Civil Procedure*, promulgated by our government. We see readable, concise documents. You don't need to take my word for it. Just follow our Supreme Court's recommendations.

Lawyers Must Communicate Effectively

Lay critics say that some lawyers have an "if you can't convince 'em, confuse 'em" game plan. They believe that there is a conscious effort to make legal documents difficult to understand, so that litigators will have plenty of work—in lawsuits trying to get a court or jury to interpret them. When people misunderstand contracts, they often breach them. Such is the stuff of which lawsuits are born.

That's the criticism that comes from nonlawyers. It's not true, but we who work in the legal field need to be aware of all sources of criticism. We need to realize that we can make many friends by using plain language. That should be reason enough for a sincere effort to write our documents in Plain English. Yet we tend to remain shackled by old, bad habits.

Legalese is one of those bad habits that has invaded the legal community. Blame it on law professors, or laziness, or poor management, or that "it's what the clients expect." The practice of using a long word when a short one will do, or using eight words when two will do, has caused some people to hate lawyers. I believe it to be a cause of lawyer-bashing. Some legal writing authorities agree (see Chapter 2).

A lawyer who uses legaldegook in talking with his client makes the client feel that he is being manipulated. A client resents receiving a copy of a pleading or other document that is so full of legalese he can't understand the overall meaning or purpose.

For these reasons, lawyer bashing is at an all-time high. The image of the lawyer must be improved. The lawyer's goal must be to communicate rather than intimidate. That process should begin with the basics.

Communication involves understanding by all parties to the communication. The power lawyers, the revolutionary thinkers, those who are in great demand, have learned that we are in the Communication Age. LAs who work for power lawyers realize that they are extensions of these lawyers. They know that the rules that apply to the lawyer apply to them as well. They make sure their actions are appropriate so they don't get the lawyer in trouble. They know how to make the lawyer look good and they take pride in doing so.

In all my teaching I try to find one little rule or guideline that will help in big ways. Learning is easy if we understand fundamentals. In writing, my most basic rule would have to be "make it easy for your reader."

Concise writing is easy on the reader. It is easily understood. It flows smoothly. It has a rhythm to it. The mind can quickly grasp its meaning. The writing doesn't get in the way. It helps the reader and is the vehicle by which our words are understood.

Flowery language is acceptable in a poem, or a novel, or other work of fiction. Shakespeare is the recognized master of the written word in his field. But is Shakespeare *easy* to understand? Do first-time Shakespeare readers "get the message" the first time through the material? I don't think so. I have to read some passages many times to understand them. I also have to stop and look up certain words. My point is that such writing has a place, it is very beautiful, and it helps us to learn. But concise, it is not.

Legal writing must be concise. We are trying to convince a judge that our side is right, and we don't have very long to do that. We often need to get our message across early, or it will be missed. Most readers don't stick around to the last page unless we have interested them on the first page—or in the first paragraph.

As you proof your work for errors, also proof it for ease of reading. Does your attention stop and start? Do you get bogged down and have to reread a passage? Do you have to stop and think about what something means? If any answers are "yes," then it's wise to revise.

Remember to write to your reader.

Canadian Trends

The Canadian Bar Association and the Canadian Bankers' Association established a Joint Committee on Plain Language Documentation in 1988. Its work is ongoing and is reported in *The Decline and Fall of Gobbledygook.*[10] The mandate of the Joint Committee provides that the committee will:

- Assess the use of English and French *plain language* in the legal profession and in the financial services industry;

- Identify barriers to the use of plain language;

- Develop one or more prototype banking documents; and

- Make recommendations relating to the greater use of plain language in legal and financial services documents.

The report presents such an excellent argument for plain language that a sane lawyer could hardly dispute it. It describes the term "legalese" as referring to "a style of writing used by lawyers that is incomprehensible to ordinary readers." The report goes on to state boldly that writing consumer contracts in legalese "greatly reduces a consumer's ability to understand the rights and duties set out in the contract." We cannot ignore this premise.

The Joint Committee agreed on these ten rules for plain language drafting:

THE TEN COMMANDMENTS FOR
PLAIN LANGUAGE DRAFTING

1.   Consider your reader and write with that reader's viewpoint in mind.

2.   Write short sentences.

3.   Say what you have to say, and no more.

4.   Use the active voice.

5.   Use simple, "everyday" words.

6.   Use words consistently.

7.   Avoid strings of synonyms.

8.   Avoid unnecessary formality.

9.   Organize your text:

      (1)   in a logical sequence,
      (2)   with informative headings, and
      (3)   with a table of contents for long documents.

10.   Make the document attractive and designed for easy reading.

Can you find any fault with those ten rules? I can't. They make sense. And what does their first rule deal with? "Consider your reader." Sadly, that many lawyers are not trained to do that.

How about number 7? Today's legal writing is full of "strings of synonyms." I immediately think of "give, devise, and bequeath," "ordered, adjudged, and decreed," "remise, release, and forever acquit," and "release, indemnify, and hold harmless." Ugh!

Endnotes

1. David Mellinkoff, *The Language of the Law* (Boston, Little Brown & Co. 1963; 11th printing 1990).

2. David Mellinkoff, *Legal Writing: Sense and Nonsense* (St. Paul, West Publishing Co., 1982).

3. David Mellinkoff, *Mellinkoff's Dictionary of American Legal Usage* (St. Paul, West Publishing Co., 1992).

4. George Hathaway, *Michigan Bar Journal*, January 1994, at 20.

5. David Mellinkoff, "Plain English in the Law," *Michigan Bar Journal*, January 1994, at 22.

6. Oliver Wendell Holmes, *The Common Law*, Lecture I.

7. Acts, 2 December 1836, 1 H. Gammel, Laws of Texas.

8. Tex. R. Civ. P. 47; *Murray v. ONA Express*, 630 S.W.2d 633 (Tex. 1982).

9. *Bader v. Cox*, 701 S.W.2d 677 (Tex. App.—Dallas 1985, writ ref'd n.r.e.).

10. *The Decline and Fall of Gobbledygook: Report on Plain Language Documentation*, Joint Committee Report of The Canadian Bar Association and The Canadian Bankers' Association, 1990.

CHAPTER 2

Advice from Lawyers and Other Legal Authorities

From the Inside Out: Mark McCormack, a Special Kind of Authority

Mark McCormack, a graduate of Yale Law School and a former associate with a large Cleveland law firm, owns a multibillion-dollar sports management business. After leaving the practice of law, he courageously wrote a "how to" book for the layman to use in dealing with lawyers. Some of his words hurt, but all of them are true.[1]

McCormack speaks both as a lawyer and a client, so he serves as excellent authority here. He tells us that much of the resentment toward lawyers is well deserved because lawyers tend to be a "real pain in the neck" and professional arrogance is an occupational hazard.

He gives some examples which will be familiar to anyone who has worked with lawyers:

- In a world where time is money, lawyers are masters at stalling.

- In business contexts, where clear communication is crucial, lawyers hide behind mumbo jumbo that nobody else understands.

- In a society where justice, in theory at least, is held up as the highest ideal, lawyers are always looking for technical and sometimes dubious means of bending the law to their advantage.

McCormack says that legalese is used as "a dodge and as a weapon, as an intimidator and as a stalling device." Legal language "conceals as much as it reveals."

But he helps us to understand lawyers by educating us about what makes them the way they are. McCormack says that lawyers are the way they are because in law school they must spend 95 percent of their time on the *technical* side of the law. The reason is obvious: the law is SO complicated. There is barely enough time to cover the extremely complex [more so every day] "letter of the law." That leaves only 5 percent of their time for learning about people and how to deal with them.

Law schools don't teach human skills. Terror is "an integral part of the law school experience," which makes it difficult for lawyers to admit when they've made an error or don't know something. Law school has taught them to "hide uncertainty at any cost." Lastly, law school has taught them "what a powerful weapon intimidation can be."

Today's lawyers are not properly taught these "bedrock lawyering skills":

- Interviewing

- Counseling

- Negotiating

- Drafting

These skills may be referred to in a syllabus but they are not properly taught. McCormack says that law school professors are brilliant men and women whose interest is in the "Black Letter Law" as written in statutes, rather than the law as it is "bent and mangled" by real life. Law school doesn't teach lawyers what they'll be doing day in, day out in their practice.

Finally, McCormack tells us that "[o]nly after graduation do young attorneys come to the depressing realization that 90 percent of what they were taught in academia will never be used in practice; and, conversely, 90 percent of what they need to know in practice was never taught to them at school."

This is alarming, but it does help the LA, as well as the layman, to understand.

In talking about excess verbiage making him angry (as a client), McCormack gives this classic example:

His company was approached to represent a hockey player who already had a contract with another agent. When McCormack saw the contract, it was handwritten on a single sheet of paper which said:

> *I, _____, hereby agree that the XYZ Agency can represent me exclusively with respect to my business activities throughout the world for a period of five years beginning January 1, 19___, and that I will pay a commission of 25% of my gross income for this service.*

McCormack sent it to his legal department for review and advice on how to void the contract. The response was that there was no way it could be voided. It was "perfectly legitimate, binding, and about as airtight as any contract ever is."

And it's under 50 words!

The LA should remember that this kind of powerful writing exists and has been successful. If we strive for this succinctness, our writing cannot help but improve. Does a client—or a judge, for that matter—really want to suffer through a lawyer's verbosity, Latin phrases, rhetorical embellishments, and pompous, ponderous paragraphs, when they add *nothing* to the meaning of the document? NO.

Legal Writing Authorities

David Mellinkoff

David Mellinkoff, that pioneer in the plain language movement to whom we owe a great debt, is law professor emeritus at the University of California at Los Angeles. He is well known in the legal field for many books and articles on the law, especially on legal writing. In his *Legal Writing: Sense and Nonsense,*[2] Professor Mellinkoff coins the word *lawsick*. What an excellent description of today's legal writing. He defines the word as a noun, an adjective, and a verb, and gives examples:

- a noun ("written in *lawsick* unclear even to its author")

- an adjective ("a *lawsick* statute")

- a verb ("the notice we prepared was *lawsicked* beyond recognition")

I think our legal writing has become lawsick. Lawyers continue to use stale, trite, wordy forms rather than thinking about what the document needs to say. I see it every day, in sentences such as this one from a pleading that recently came across my desk:

> *BE IT REMEMBERED that on the 30th day of March, 19xx, came on for hearing before this Honorable Court the motion of Plaintiff to Supplement XYZ Corporation's Appendix to Plaintiff's Memorandum of Points and Authorities in Support of Motion for Summary Judgment, and this Court being of the opinion that such Motion is well taken and should be granted, does hereby grant the motion of Plaintiff to Supplement XYZ Corporation's Appendix to Plaintiff's Memorandum of Points and Authorities in Support of Motion for Summary Judgment.*

That's a pretty sick sentence. In the first place, the document needed only a short title, such as "XYZ's Motion to Supplement Appendix." The order needed to say only that "XYZ's appendix is supplemented to include [whatever it requested in the motion]," be dated and signed.

We should follow Professor Mellinkoff's "Seven Rules," where he discusses:

1. Peculiar: The language of the law is more peculiar than precise, but "don't confuse peculiarity with precision."

2. Precise: The price of sloppy writing is misunderstanding and creative misinterpretation.

3. English: Follow the rules of English composition.

4. Clear: Choose clarity.

5. Law: Write law simply. Do not puff, mangle, or hide.

6. Plan: Before you write, plan.

7. Cut: Cut it in half!

Mellinkoff's books should be required reading in every law school They also should be readily available in every firm law library. They are appearing in more places now, but not nearly enough. Everyone who works in law offices should be aware of the plain language movement and of the need for concise writing in legal documents. We need constant reminders from such outstanding authorities as Professor Mellinkoff.

Professor Mellinkoff's works gave birth to the legal plain language movement; the banner is being carried by some outstanding members of the legal community. I have included a few of the more prominent here, so you will have the benefit of their wisdom.

Joseph Kimble

Joseph Kimble, a professor at the Thomas M. Cooley Law School in Lansing, Michigan, is probably the premier advocate for clear writing in the American legal community today. He edits the *Plain Language* column for the *Michigan Bar Journal*. Professor Kimble has written a comprehensive law review article entitled *Plain English: A Charter for*

Clear Writing.[3] This should be required reading for every lawyer and every LA.

Professor Kimble is an active member of the Legal Writing Institute, founded at the University of Puget Sound School of Law in 1984. The institute has more than 850 members in the United States and Canada, publishes a newsletter[4] and a journal, and holds a three-day conference every other year. At the 1990 conference of the Institute in Ann Arbor, Kimble submitted the following resolution, which the conference adopted:

RESOLUTION

At the 1990 conference of the Legal Writing Institute, which has 900 members worldwide, the participants adopted the following resolution:

1. The way lawyers write has been a source of complaint about lawyers for more than four centuries.

2. The language used by lawyers should agree with the common speech, unless there are reasons for a difference.

3. Legalese is unnecessary and no more precise than plain language.

4. Plain language is an important part of good legal writing.

5. Plain language means language that is clear and readily understandable to the intended readers.

6. To encourage the use of plain language, the Legal Writing Institute should try to identify members in each state and in Canada who would be willing to work with their bar associations to establish plain language committees like those in Michigan and Texas.

The State Bar of Michigan was the first to organize a plain language Committee. (Never underestimate the power of what just a few people can do.) Michigan was followed closely by Texas, and now by Missouri.

California adopted a resolution in favor of plain language, and perhaps that work will rise to the level of a state bar committee. The trend is clear.

Nine states have statutes requiring consumer documents to be written in plain language. Lawyers who hold on to "tradition" in their writing will soon be swimming upstream. Although they have company in great numbers, they are still bucking an unmistakably clear trend.

Kimble correctly insists that plain English must "start in law school and be carried unstintingly to practicing lawyers," but adds that his former students complain that their new employer "doesn't want it that way."[5] He must agree with Mark McCormack's view that the roots of the problem are in law school, as he quotes Professor John Lindsey: "Lawyers suffer from a 'chronic ailment' because they are 'continuously exposed to law books, the largest body of poorly written literature ever created by the human race.'"[6]

Sage advice from Kimble includes the following, from a list of more than 30 elements of plain English:

1. Avoid legal jargon.

2. Avoid unnecessary Latin *(arguendo, inter alia)*.

3. Avoid doublets and triplets *(any and all; give, devise, and bequeath)*.

4. Omit unnecessary detail.

5. Prefer short and medium-length sentences.

6. Avoid intrusive phrases; keep the subject near the verb, and the verb near the object.

7. Avoid multiple negatives.

8. Be consistent; use the same term for the same thing, without guilt.[7]

He asks that we use a style we would use if our readers were "sitting across the table, and [we] wanted to make sure they understood."[8] Exploding all the myths about plain English, Kimble says that "legalese and traditional style persist for the same reasons as always—habit, inertia, fear of change, the overwhelming influence of poor models, the rote use of forms, and notions of self-interest (prestige and control). Not to mention lack of skill."[9]

I believe that if we could just clone Professor Kimble and install those clones in every law school, we could attend the Grand Funeral for Legalese very soon. If his law review article were required reading for law students, law professors, and all lawyers, life in the legal community would improve, as would the lawyer's image outside the legal community.

David C. Elliott

David C. Elliott, a prominent barrister and solicitor in Edmonton, Alberta, is another strong supporter of plain language. His efforts are well known in Canada and he belongs to the Legal Writing Institute and other plain language groups.

Counselor Elliott has written "A Model Plain-Language Act,"[10] which calls for monetary penalties in a schedule called the "Gobbledygook Fee Scale." The fines are repeated for each use and if used more than ten times in a document, they are *trebled*. With his permission, I reprint:

Gobbledygook Fee Scale

For each	Amount
above-captioned	$ 100
above-referenced	100
above-said	100
A.D. (Anno Domini)	1,000
aforementioned	150
aforesaid	150
and/or	200
beforementioned	100
came on for consideration	100
come(s) now	200
hath	100
hereby	100
herein	125
hereinabove	150

hereinbefore	200
hereinbelow	150
hereunto	150
inasmuch as	100
inter alia	100
know all men by these presents	200
now come(s)	200
ordered, adjudged, and decreed	100
pursuant to	100
said *(for the, this, these, or those)*	150
saith	75
same (as pronoun)	175
sayeth	75
ss	100
such *(for the, this, these, or those)*	150
therefor	150
thereunto	100
to wit	150
viz.	150
wherefore	150
wherein	100
whereof	100
witnesseth	200

Amen! I've seen some pleadings that would be fined $10,000 under this schedule of fines. I wish it could be put into effect. We should impose it on ourselves.

Bryan Garner

Bryan Garner is a Texas lawyer who now devotes all of his time to helping others write well. He is one of my champions—a real pioneer in the plain language movement. Through his Dallas-based LawProse Inc., he offers workshops and institutes in advanced legal drafting, writing, and editing.

Oxford University Press published Garner's *A Dictionary of Modern Legal Usage*[11] in 1987, followed in 1991 by his *The Elements of Legal Style*[12]. His books should be on your desks. Every lawyer should have *The Elements of Legal Style* nearby, just as journalists and other writers keep Strunk & White[13] nearby.

Garner's rules encompass all that we are told by all concise writing experts, but in his chapter 5, "Words and Expressions Confused and Misused," he has compiled a list of terms we see every day that we must delete from our legal writing. You must make sure both you and your lawyers read and learn that chapter.

I list some of them here. (This is a partial listing. Please read Garner's book for the complete list and the explanations.) How many have you seen, countless times, in legal writing? It will take serious concentration to strike these terms from your vocabulary and your writing, but strike them you must.

Strike from Your Vocabulary

aforementioned	if and when	refer back
aforesaid	implement	remand back
above-mentioned,	interface	res gestae
above-listed	in terms of	said
and/or	make reference to	[as an adjective]
arguendo	null and void	same [as a
as far as . . . is	numerous	pronoun]
concerned	on the part of	such
before-mentioned	overly	[for this, these,
commence	parameters	or the]
deem	preliminary to	thereof
each and every	preparatory to	therein
enclosed	preventative	thereout
please find	previous to	utilize
herein	prioritize	whereas
hereinafter	prior to	whereof
hereinafter called	provided that	wherefore
hereinbefore	pursuant to	wherein
herewith	reason . . . is	
hopefully	because	

Other Legal Writing Authorities

West Publishing Company, a premier legal publisher, publishes a series of books in its "In a Nutshell" series. *Legal Writing in a Nutshell*[14] tells us to "omit archaic legalisms," such as *hereinafter, heretofore, aforesaid, forthwith, herein, hereby, for purposes hereof, notwithstanding anything to the contrary herein, by these presents,* and *said.* The authors call them "obstacles to the lay reader" and "imprecise and thus troublesome to the legal reader." The book effectively invites us to organize our thinking and shorten our sentences.

Some of my readers might think, "What will we substitute if we eliminate these archaic legalisms?" Well, most of the time we don't need a substitute. But here are some suggestions:

Instead of "quoted hereinafter," say "quoted on page 18."

Instead of "heretofore sent to you," say "sent to you on July 8."

Instead of "said accident," say "the accident."

Instead of "as aforesaid," say "as stated in paragraph 9."

Instead of "notwithstanding anything to the contrary herein," say nothing. If your document contains contrary and conflicting provisions or any provisions needing this phrase, you'd best rewrite them, period.

Get the idea? Just speak plainly and concisely. Think of your reader. Write the way you speak as much as you can. In conversation, do you say "enclosed herewith please find the scarf I borrowed"? No, you say, "I'm returning your scarf," or simply "Here's your scarf." In your everyday speaking, do you say, "Whereupon, I went to the store"? No. You say, "Then I went to the store."

Steve Albrecht has written a useful book for the LA entitled *The Paralegal's Desk Reference.*[15] In a section entitled "Better Legal Writing" (at page 114), he quotes a "wise old humorist" as saying, "Lawyers are the only people who can write a 10,000-word document and call it a 'brief.'" He goes on to state that the "often misguided attempt to write like others in the legal profession usually leads to poor writing habits that create documents neither clients, judges, nor even other attorneys can understand." Albrecht repeats what we hear from a growing list of experts: "Who is the reader?" He cautions us to avoid legal jargon and to prepare our thoughts—especially when our writing is going to be read by nonlegal people. That usually includes the client, doesn't it?

Three of the best books for the LA who works in litigation are *The Litigation Paralegal*[16] by Eastern Kentucky University professor James W. H. McCord; *Manual for the Lawyer's Assistant*,[17] by the National Association of Legal Secretaries; and *Paralegal Practice and Procedure*, by Deborah E. Larbalestrier[18]. Every competent LA who works in litigation should have access to these works—not because they advocate plain language but because of their general usefulness in litigation.

Others in the legal community who are fueling the plain language trend in earnest are Robert A. Esperti and Renno L. Peterson. They are practicing estate planning attorneys who are training "Loving Trust" attorneys to help clients with estate planning documents they can understand. Their clients love it and their business is bursting. Their first book was *Loving Trust*.[19] That book was written in plain language and is layman-readable. Their latest version combined that book with *The Living Trust Revolution*, which contains forms and sample language to be used in estate planning documents—all in plain English.

In my research for this book, I came across a West Publishing Company book entitled *Case Analysis and Fundamentals of Legal Writing*.[20] In this textbook, Statsky and Wernet comment on judicial opinions with a section entitled "Many Opinions Are Poorly Written."[21] Statsky asked participants at a judicial conference to comment on judicial opinions and received the following criticisms:

"Opinions are too long."

"They tend to ramble."

"They conceal the issues."

"They fail to speak in plain words."

"They are filled with 'legalese.'"

And that's what our lawyers spend most of their time reading. See? McCormack is right. It's no wonder our lawyers are off track and don't write concisely. We must do what *we* can in drafting pleadings for them. The work we do for them should be concise, informative, and written in *plain language*.

A Famous Trial Lawyer

John M. O'Quinn is a Houston lawyer famous for multiple multimillion-dollar verdicts in complex cases. He teaches other lawyers from time to time in seminars.[22] When talking about jury selection, he says he rewrites his voir dire "until I can make a 12-year-old understand it in ten minutes and say it back to me." He literally tries it out on a 12-year-old and if that 12-year-old understands the issues in his case, O'Quinn has done what he intended. He knows the jury will understand. That strategy is built on the same premise as writing with your reader in mind. Make your writing easy for your reader to understand. Help your reader, as O'Quinn helps his jurors.

O'Quinn is a brilliant lawyer with a photographic memory, who was first in his law school class and scored highest on the bar exam. From about 1979 through 1994 he lost only one jury trial, while winning about $1.5 *billion* for his cients. Jurors like him and trust him, and his cases bring hundreds of millions of dollars to his plaintiff-clients. One of the ways he does it is by using *simple language*. He is also organized and well prepared. That behavior is *learned*, through practice, practice, practice. We don't need to be born a MENSA. We can learn how to persuade others that we are right—the goal of most of our legal writing.

A Jury Consultant

Noelle C. Nelson, a clinical psychologist and prominent jury consultant, has written *A Winning Case*[23] to help lawyers communicate with juries and win lawsuits. In the chapter on "How to Satisfy the Jurors' Need for Logic," she lists five techniques to ensure that the trial lawyer's use of language helps rather than hurts his case. They are:

1. Speak everyday language.

2. Avoid jargon or legalese. (Using jargon makes the jurors feel like outcasts, that they're not part of the "in group.")

3. Phrase for clarity of thought. (Phrase your ideas one thought at a time.)

4. Get to the point. (It's tragic to lose a valid case simply because you are not understood.)

5. Check your speech. (How easy to understand is your vocabulary?)

These five rules apply to our written words as well. Whether we do our selling to a judge, to a jury, to the client, to our opponent, or to a management committee, we must be understood. Our logic must be followed, and we must win. Think of the clients. The clients must be proud of what we are doing for them or they won't be back—nor will they refer others.

Endnotes

1. Mark H. McCormack, *The Terrible Truth About Lawyers*, Mark H. McCormack Enterprises, Inc., 1987, Beech Tree Books, William Morrow & Co., New York; reprinted by Avon Books, a division of The Hearst Corporation, New York 1988, subtitled *What I Should Have Learned at Yale Law School*.

2. David Mellinkoff, *Legal Writing: Sense and Nonsense* (St. Paul, West Publishing Company, 1992).

3. Joseph Kimble, *Plain English: A Charter for Clear Writing*, 9 Thomas M. Cooley L. Rev. 1 (1992).

4. *The Second Draft*, prepared at Boston College Law School by Joan Blum, Jane Gionfriddo, and Francine Sherman.

5. *Id.* at 30.

6. *Id.* at 9, quoting John M. Lindsey, *The Legal Writing Malady: Causes and Cures*, N.Y.L.J. Dec. 12, 1990, at 2.

7. *Id.* at 12-14.

8. *Id.* at 19.

9. *Id.* at 22.

10. David C. Elliott, "A Model Plain-Language Act," reprinted with permission of the *Texas Bar Journal*, December 1993, Volume 56, page 1118.

11. Bryan A. Garner, *A Dictionary of Modern Legal Usage* (New York, Oxford University Press, Inc., 1987).

12. Bryan A. Garner, *The Elements of Legal Style* (New York, Oxford University Press, Inc., 1991).

13. William Strunk Jr. and E. B. White, *The Elements of Style*, 3d ed. (New York, Macmillan Publishing Co., 1979).

14. Lynn B. Squires and Marjorie Dick Rombauer, *Legal Writing in a Nutshell* (St. Paul, West Publishing Company, 1982).

15. Steve Albrecht, *The Paralegal's Desk Reference* (Englewood Cliffs, Prentice Hall, Inc., 1993).

16. James W. H. McCord, *The Litigation Paralegal, A Systems Approach*, 2d ed. (St. Paul, West Publishing Company, 1992).

17. National Association of Legal Secretaries, *Manual for the Lawyer's Assistant*, 3d ed. (St. Paul, West Publishing Company, 1994).

18. Deborah E. Larbalestrier, *Paralegal Practice and Procedure,* 2d ed. (Englewood Cliffs, N.J., Prentice Hall, Inc., 1986).

19. Robert A. Esperti and Renno L. Peterson, *Loving Trust* (New York, Penguin Books, 1991).

20. William P. Statsky and R. John Wernet, Jr., *Case Analysis and Fundamentals of Legal Writing* (St. Paul, West Publishing Company, 1984).

21. *Id.* at 86-87.

22. John M. O'Quinn, "The Art of Jury Selection: Plaintiff's Techniques" (1994).

23. Noelle C. Nelson, *A Winning Case* (Englewood Cliffs, Prentice Hall, Inc., 1991).

CHAPTER 3

Advice from the Government

Legislation

Professor Kimble, in his law review article,[1] has prepared a comprehensive list of the work being done in business, government, law, and education, including federal and state legislation requiring consumer statutes to be written in plain language. You will recognize a few of those federal statutes already passed:

- Truth in Lending Act, 15 U.S.C. §§ 1601-65b (1988)

- Real Estate Settlement Procedures Act, 12 U.S.C. § 1681 (1988)

- Magnuson-Moss Warranty-Federal Trade Commission Improvement Act, 15 U.S.C. §§ 2301-12 (1988)

On October 13, 1994, Arthur Leavitt, Chairman of the Securities & Exchange Commission, publicly challenged mutual funds to write their prospectuses in plain English, with a plain English summary right in front, so that investors can understand them. He said that they then would be approved more quickly by the SEC. Chairman Leavitt observed that in their efforts at full disclosure they have created documents that are "more redundant than revealing."

I suspect that this is exactly what has created this legal writing problem we have—efforts at full disclosure. Or, put another way, efforts to make our work all-inclusive. There is fear that a pleading will be stricken or a case thrown out because some insignificant word or phrase has been omitted. Sadly, that has happened in the past.

But now we are more sophisticated, as are clients, judges, and juries. Every sentence in a document does not need to ward off every possible contingency. Words do not need to be defined twelve times. Communication is easy if we don't make it difficult.

In your pleadings and other legal documents, if you're speaking of the Central Des Moines Savings Bank, call it "Bank." If you mean the verb "use," don't say "utilize"; if you mean "before," don't say "preliminary to." If you mean "these documents," don't say "said documents." And if you mean "if," don't use "in the event that."

Judicial Training

The Federal Judicial Center in Washington was established by Congress in 1967 (28 U.S.C. §§ 620-29). One of its mandates is to provide training for the judiciary—that includes training in writing. The Center also keeps up with technology and performs research in areas affecting our courts.

The center is chaired by the Chief Justice of the United States Supreme Court and publishes the Judicial Writing Manual to "serve the cause of good opinion writing." Since the "link between courts and the public is the written word," the "burden of the judicial opinion is to explain and to persuade and to satisfy the world that the decison is principled and sound. What the court says, *and how it says it*, is as important as what the court decides." (My emphasis.)

The manual lists five characteristics of bad writing. The explanations are scathing. It matters not that the manual is directed to judges. Its teachings are for *all* of us. Do you recognize any of these flaws from your attorney's (or your own) legal writing?

Wordiness: Not just using two words when one will do, but trying to convey too much information, covering too many issues, and simply writing too much. Often wordiness reflects the writer's failure (or inability) to separate the material from the immaterial and do the grubby work of editing.

Lack of precision and clarity: "Some legal writers lack the ability to write simple, straightforward prose." This may be because "the writer is not sure of a legal principle or of how to state it precisely." Condemning bad thought, the manual goes on: "the word is no better than the thought from which it springs." The solution? "Painstaking and thoughtful editing is essential for precise writing."

Poor organization: Closely related to lack of precision. The organization "will be a road map enabling the reader to follow from the beginning to the end without getting lost." Notice the advice we have from many of the experts referred to in this book: *enabling the reader to follow*. We must give more attention to the reader. Can you follow every opinion you read? Can you do it with your lawyers' writings? I've had trouble following even one paragraph. More so when that entire paragraph is one sentence!

Cryptic analysis: If our writing "omits steps in the reasoning essential to understanding," it will "fail to serve its purposes."

Pomposity and humor: It's not only judicial writing that can be pompous. Responses, whether in the form of an appellee's brief or to a motion for summary judgment, can be not only pompous but condescending in tone. Humor is often lost in sarcasm. The manual says that while some judges have succeeded with humor, "it works better in after-dinner speeches than in judicial opinions." The manual makes the salient point that the litigants are "not likely to see anything funny in the litigation." I certainly don't want to criticize humor, because when it's proper, there's nothing better. I only want you to refrain from being sarcastic or emotional in drafting your legal documents. It does not wear well.

The manual then offers some guides for good writing, referring us to Strunk & White[2], a book that should be on every desk. It concentrates on matters of style and stresses rules that we need frequently in our writing. It's not a large volume with a gigantic index, but a useful little style book. It is the journalist's constant companion. It should be yours as well. (And with any reference to Strunk & White, I must refer you to Bryan Garner's book on *legal* style: *The Elements of Legal Style.*[3])

But back to the government manual: Guess what's Number One on the government manual's list? *Write plain English!*

Much work is being done to rewrite pattern jury instructions, and the Federal Judicial Center is helping in that regard. The Fifth and Sixth Circuits' committees on pattern jury instructions follow the Federal Judicial Center's instructions. The Eighth and Ninth Circuits' committees recommend plain language. The State Bar of Michigan spent three years in revising jury instructions in plain English. Texas is in a massive revision. Oregon, Iowa, and Missouri are revising jury instructions to be better understood, with rules such as:

- Use short sentences

- Use the active voice

- Avoid negatives

- Use simple, understandable words

Judge Lynn Hughes: One Federal Judge's Fight

What are some of the specific topics on which we can concentrate in our fight for conciseness and clarity? Some are: referring to the parties, dealing with numbers, describing actions, matters involving groups, capitalization, recitations, and needless words in general.

In the Southern District of Texas, United States District Judge Lynn N. Hughes's local rules *require* plain language. That doesn't mean it's suggested or preferred, but required. He has stricken pleadings that contain gobbledygook and don't make sense. He is chairman of the Plain Language Committee of the State Bar of Texas. He has had an effect; the

Southern District of Texas has formally endorsed the use of plain language in court.

If all lawyers would follow his rules—even a few of them—we too would champion the cause against legalese. We would see real communication going on; all parties to a lawsuit would understand the documents being filed on their behalf.

Judge Hughes's rules will sound familiar to you, now that we have reviewed some other plain language proponents' works, but we can never get enough reinforcement. With his permission, I reprint from his local rules:

LOCAL RULES OF
UNITED STATES DISTRICT COURT FOR THE
SOUTHERN DISTRICT OF TEXAS, HOUSTON DIVISION
LYNN HUGHES, DISTRICT JUDGE

The most valuable of all talents is
never using two words when one will do.
Thomas Jefferson

1. Capitalize only proper nouns. Never capitalize whole words.

2. Do not use roman numerals. [Judge Hughes once quipped in a seminar: "If you're so fond of roman numerals, send your clients' bills in roman numerals!"]

3. List in columns series of more than three dates, names or numbers. [This suggestion will help your pleadings considerably. Your writing will be noticed.]

4. Adopt short, clear labels for the parties.

   A. Use part of their name (Acme Consolidated Bank & Trust Co. = Acme), or
   B. Use their real-world capacity (Acme Consolidated Bank & Trust Co. = bank);
   C. Do not use their lawsuit capacity (plaintiff, respondent).

5. Be concrete, not abstract: car wreck, not vehicular collision.

6. Caption the document helpfully.

    A. Exxon's Answer
    B. USF&G's Motion for Summary Judgment
    C. Allied's Cross Action against Chase

7. Omit needless words.

    A. **Never use**:

    (1) said (as an article)
    (2) cause for case or action
    (3) to wit
    (4) same (as a pronoun)
    (5) and/or
    (6) hereby, herein, whereas, thereof, etc.

    B. Say it once, right; **do not say**:

    (1) each and every
    (2) on or about (around)
    (3) by and through
    (4) ordered, adjudged, and decreed

    C. **Avoid** tautologies, like:

    (1) past history
    (2) mutual agreement
    (3) reason why
    (4) total sum

    D. **Eliminate** stale, useless formalisms, like:

    (1) comes now
    (2) be it remembered that

    E. Delete fluff:

    (1) in accordance with the terms and conditions of = under
    (2) pursuant to = under
    (3) attorney's fees *in the amount of* = attorney's fees of

(4) to and including = through
(5) on or before = by

Notice 7C: "Avoid tautologies." The word "tautology" is not exactly "plain English," is it? What is a tautology, that weird animal so prevalent in legal writing that Judge Hughes felt it necessary to include in his local rules?

In *Write Tight*,[4] Brohaugh defines a tautology as more than a repetition or redundancy. He calls it a "superfluous repetition," and lists examples: small smidgeon, annual birthday, glowing ember, pure unadulterated truth, itsy bitsy spider, protrude out, rise up, dash quickly, cash money, switchblade knife, each and every, forever and ever, the one and only.

Whew! Do you now understand what a tautology is? And can you think of hundreds we see every day in legal documents?

And/Or Deserves Special Recognition

Go back to number 5 under 7A: "and/or." It's everywhere in legal writing, isn't it? Perhaps there are *some* cases where it *might* be acceptable, but I doubt it. Try your best never to use this bit of legalese. Lawyers use "and/or" with no thought of whether it's necessary. They think that surely "and/or" covers all the bases. Well, that's not the case, and the use of "and/or" could just lose a case for you.

An international organization named CLARITY is a movement to simplify legal language. It publishes a journal with news and articles from its worldwide plain-language-afficionado members. The October 1994 issue has an article listing cases where the use of "and/or" in the pleadings was fatal. The article describes the use of "and/or" as "often absurd, fequently disastrous, and always unnecessary."

For your review, here are some of those cases:

Vilando v. County of Sacramento, 54 Cal. App. 2d 413, 129 P.2d 165 (1942). The phrase "officer and/or agent" was not affirmative that he was an agent of the county; case dismissed.

Sproule v. Taffe, 294 Ill. App. 374, 13 N.E.2d 827 (1938). Default judgment voided because it was unclear who owned the lease (pleaded as

"Sproule *and/or Fidelity Life Ins. Co.*" Before ruling that "[a] judgment not designating in whose favor it is rendered is void for uncertainty," the court wrote in living color:

> We have many times condemned in unmeasured terms the use of "and/or" as a "confusing fad," "accuracy destroying symbol," "pollution of the English language," that "barbarism," "unsightly hieroglyphic," "verbal teratism," and other terms of a similar character that we could think of up to this time. (Citations omitted.) Many courts of other jurisdictions have, in like terms, condemned the use of this symbol (citations omitted).

The court also made this statement: "We think we ought to say that counsel for plaintiff or plaintiffs state they had no part in drawing the lease."

Shadden v. Cowan, 213 Georgia 29, 96 S.E.2d 608 (1957). The equivocal term "taxpayers and/or patrons" did not properly state plaintiffs' right to bring the action.

Underhill v. Alameda Elem. School Dist., 133 Cal. App. 733, 24 P.2d 849 (1933). Trial court upheld on appeal in dismissing complaint where it had been alleged that the plaintiff was taking part in a game "and/or" playing in the immediate vicinity of the game. The court said: "We deem it appropriate to call attention to the confusion brought about by the misuse of the term 'and/or.'"

I have seen a few—*very* few—times when *and/or* is acceptable. Recently, in preparing an order for probate court that involved distributions from two different trusts, the drafting attorney didn't know if distributions would be made from both trusts because the accounting information wasn't complete. The sentence therefore stated that distributions would be made from "Trust 1 and/or Trust 2." (I couldn't talk her out of it, and I had to admit, it was probably an exception.)

A final rule from Judge Hughes is: "Omit recitations in orders. Whether it is a final judgment or a housekeeping order, keep it bare and decisional. Omit all recitations." (*All* recitations means *all* recitations.)

On that subject, here are some quotations from case law: "The issue does appear complicated by an extensive 'Final Decree' and contemporaneous repetitive 'Order,' both containing extensive recitals, in violation of the Federal Rules." *Petrol Corp. v. Petroleum Heat & Power Co.*, 162 F.2d 327, 328 (2d Cir. 1947).

And: "[i]n America the decree does not ordinarily recite either the bill or answer or pleadings, and generally not the facts on which the decree is founded." *Whiting v. Bank of the United States*, 38 U.S. 6, 13 Pet. R. 13, 14 (1839) (Story).

The United States Supreme Court is the law of the land, the only court created by the United States Constitution, the court of last resort, the Final Word. Yet the United States Supreme Court *in 1839* told us not to make recitations in orders, and lawyers are still doing it!

I quote from an order signed by Judge Hughes in a case where the plaintiff's lawyer's writing was less than desirable in major ways. Here was Judge Hughes's advice in the form of an order:

> [Plaintiff] will file a two-page bill of particulars describing the claims against [defendant] and the date the claims arose. She will file another two-page bill of particulars describing the underlying facts showing [bank's] involvement. She will file a two-page brief explaining why claims against a reorganized debtor are not barred by discharge in bankruptcy. Proponents of federal jurisdiction must file a two-page, precise memorandum on exactly what questions must be determined in federal court rather than pleaded as an affirmative defense in state court.

> These instruments will have no words in all capitals, will not use the expression *and/or*, will not lack precision in fact and law or otherwise convey the lawyer's inability to communicate.

When I first saw that order, I shrieked, "YES!" This is a strong order. Any lawyer would understand what is expected from such clear instructions. Look at the words Judge Hughes uses to describe what he wants: "precise," "exactly," and "communicate." Oh, yes, and "two-page."

Judge Hughes also marks up proposed orders submitted to him. Each of those marked-up orders is a vital lesson for any attorney practicing in his (or anybody's) court. It's meant to teach. For example, in another case in Judge Hughes's court a lawyer submitted the following order on an unopposed motion to designate attorney in charge:

> IT IS HEREBY ORDERED that Plaintiffs' Unopposed
> Motion to Substitute Counsel is GRANTED. [Name] is
> hereby substituted as Attorney-in-Charge for Plaintiffs.
>
> SIGNED THIS ____ day of _____, 1990.

Judge Hughes marked it up, signed it, and stamped it, and the final,
Hughes-edited version read:

> On the plaintiffs' unopposed motion, [Name] is
> substituted as attorney in charge for the plaintiffs.
>
> August 19, 1990.

From 30 words to 18 words. From needless, superfluous, distracting
capital letters to a free-flowing, easily read and understood sentence. We
have no need for capitalization if our words are chosen wisely.

But Judge Hughes, or any judge for that matter, should not have to
explain it to lawyers as if they were kindergarteners. Lawyers should
clean up their own writing without being told to do so in the middle of
a lawsuit.

Motions

The more complicated the motion, the more necessary that it be in
plain language. Judge Hughes gives an excellent *structure* of a legal
argument:

> *X is true because*
> *A, B, and C are true.*

If your motions have this structure, they will be winners. If you
cannot build your motion from this structure, there is something wrong
with either your premise or your writing. Work on it.

Judge Hughes frequently presents seminars on "Effective Motion
Drafting Techniques," proposing:

4 Steps to a Successful Motion

1. Think. No document can rise above the thought that created it.

2. Tell the court what you want—briefly and clearly.

3. Tell the court why you ought to get it—briefly and clearly, legally and factually.

4. Furnish an order granting that *specific* relief (not merely granting the motion).

He also advises lawyers to say something useful right at the start. Judge Hughes says, "the first hundred words of virtually every court paper are pointless recitations and deleterious formalisms." He says we should summarize the document in 35 or fewer words and start strong. He adds that "many judges will not get past the first 50 words, so use them well."

It's not only judges who need to become interested in the first 50 words. Our clients should not have to wade through legalese, with *Black's Law Dictionary* close at hand. They should be able to understand what we have written and say "Yes!" or "All right!" or "Now you're talkin'!" Why don't we make those clients proud of us? Why don't we make them our number one fans?

Why should we make it difficult to *communicate* with the clients? We don't have to make all sentences short and choppy; we don't have to write so that a zombie could understand. But we do need to write clearly. If any intended reader does not understand our writing, we have failed.

Summary

So, added to our arsenal is the government and the judiciary fighting for plain language, fighting for lawyers to *think*, and fighting for better communication. I am optimistic, and I am committed to the fight for plain language. You will be, too, because after you work with plain language principles for a while, the legalese and noncommunicative mumbo-jumbo will make you wonder what appeal it can hold.

After you practice on some pleadings, edit some of the documents that cross your desk, and streamline your own documents, you will soon cringe when you see legalese.

Of course, any hope for big change from this book comes backed by powerful optimism. But it's one more door to enter, opening on one more arena to fight the fight. Great legal minds are carrying one banner; the government is carrying one, too; and we LAs should as well. It's just the right thing to do. There are learned government and lay experts who agree. The work has begun with lawyers and is proceeding deliberately, if slowly. It must also begin with us. The effective LA must know how to draft pleadings, even if only the general ones. The LA can help keep the lawyer from getting into trouble with judges. The LA can help the lawyer to communicate effectively with clients, too.

Endnotes

1. Joseph Kimble, "Plain English: A Charter for Clear Writing" (Thomas M. Cooley Law Review, Vol. 9, No. 1, 1992).

2. William Strunk Jr. & E. B. White, *The Elements of Style*, 3d ed., (New York, Macmillan Publishing Co., Inc., 1979).

3. Bryan A. Garner, *The Elements of Legal Style* (New York, Oxford University Press, 1991).

4. William Brohaugh, *Write Tight* (Cincinnati, Writer's Digest Books, 1993).

CHAPTER 4

Advice from
General Writing Authorities

The Elements of Style is a famous reference work, the foremost authority on style for many writers and journalists. Commonly referred to as Strunk & White,[1] it was originally written by a professor at Cornell University, William Strunk Jr. His "short, valuable essay on the nature and beauty of brevity" begins: "Vigorous writing is concise. A sentence should contain no unnecessary words, a paragraph no unnecessary sentences." He says that a writer should be required to "make all his sentences short."

The White of Strunk & White is E. B. White, a student of Professor Strunk, who wrote revisions for the later editions and became a famous author in his own right. Strunk & White has stood the test of time and

45

Litigation LAs should memorize the fourth chapter, "Words and Expressions Commonly Misused."

Another useful book is Jan Venolia's *Write Right!*[2] Ms. Venolia has written an excellent, concise desktop reference, and the latest printing contains the results of her research on changes in our language. She makes this important point: "[G]ood writing today strives to make the reader's job easier, clearing away distracting clutter and obstacles." She is fond of quotes, and shares this one from Mark Twain: "Writing is easy. All you have to do is cross out the wrong words."

A recent bestseller mentioned in chapter 3 is William Brohaugh's *Write Tight*[3], in which he suggests that "tight writing makes its point." Brohaugh says that tight writing is "the difference between hitting with a pillow and hitting with a baseball bat." He calls pillow writing flabby and boring, unsure, evasive, and disrespectful to the reader. But baseball-bat writing "shows confidence and communicates authority."

Brohaugh lists 16 types of wordiness and explains how to avoid them. One of those suggestions hits lawyers hard: "Eliminate the 'deadwould,'" quoting from Joe Floren in *Write Smarter, Not Harder*. The unnecessary "would" is a mainstay of bad pleading form. How often have you seen in a pleading: "Plaintiff would show . . . ."? Or, "Defendant would state to the court as follows:"? Well, the question is, *when* would plaintiff or defendant show whatever he's going to show? What purpose does that "would" serve?

Brohaugh also derides the use of jargon, consistently long sentences, repetitive construction, clichés, vogue words, and overkill—all found in abundance in legal writing.

"Probably it won't be easy for you to express yourself in short, simple words. You say them every day, but they don't come to you when you sit down to write," predicted Dr. Rudolf Flesch.[4] Dr. Flesch, who gave us *The Art of Plain Talk* and *Why Johnny Can't Read & What You Can Do About It*, reminds us that *simplicity* is the key to for successful communication. He describes average sentence length in words from Very Easy (8 words or less) to Very Difficult (29 or more), with "Difficult" being at 25 words per sentence and "Standard" at 17.[5] Dr. Flesch advises that we "learn to cut," because: "The most common fault of writing is wordiness; the most important editorial job is cutting."[6]

In all my years of working for lawyers, I have rarely found them to cut. More often, they *add* words in revising. That's fine when the added words are necessary. But sometimes they are used just to fill up a page or extend a paragraph. This shows a lack of confidence. They're just not sure they've exhausted their knowledge of the subject, so they throw in more. Or they're just not sure they've really convinced the audience. Or they anticipate way too many possible arguments, most of which are never raised.

Legal writing is just a specialized form of business writing. I recommend that you study *Plain Style*, by Richard Lauchman.[7] LAs need this book as a reference; purchase it for your library.

Lauchman says that business writing should have an "invisible" style which "must never create needless complexity," with every expression being "functional." He describes management's review process as being a "minefield," with manager after manager exploding the text. "Each successive manager," Lauchman writes, "believing he's not doing his job unless he improves the writing in some way (or merely wishing to impose a personal stamp), alters a phrase, substitutes a word, adds a sentence, or qualifies an expression."

That reminds me of the process in law firms where an associate prepares a document and it then goes up through the ranks to the partner who will be signing off on it. By the time it's done, it's a lasting tribute to unreadability. Lauchman uses this example: "The honest and simple [word] *policy* is changed to the less precise *procedure* and then to the imprecise but impressive *protocol*." Any LA who has experience with lawyers has first-hand knowledge of this drill. If you are doing *any* drafting of legal documents, please read Mr. Lauchman's book in addition to the legal authorities I have cited. His chapter on conciseness is one of the best I've seen. Every lawyer in America should read this book. Maybe an effective LA can influence a lawyer or two to read it.

Mary A. DeVries has written about a dozen books on effective writing and communications. As our world becomes smaller and our marketplace becomes global, lawyers must begin to think internationally. One of Ms. DeVries' latest offerings is *Internationally Yours*,[8] subtitled "Writing and Communicating Successfully in Today's Global Market-place." The LA needs this book in working with lawyers who have international clients or do any work in other countries. In advising on customs and practices, message design, style, and "language demons," she also cautions us to "say—in very simple, straightforward language—exactly what you mean." Further, the "best advice is to make it short and keep it simple." Finally, she cautions us to remember this general rule, which I believe deserves to stand apart and receive added attention:

> Any sentence that has more than twenty words
> is difficult to understand.

In 1981 Professor Robert C. Pinckert wrote an entertaining guide to the English language and effective communication entitled *The Truth About English*[9]. Professor Pinckert discusses formal and informal English, how to choose our words, and how to construct good sentences and paragraphs. He then goes on to show us how to *persuade* in a *pleasing style*. He says there aren't any wrong words. "There are wrong uses of words." He strikes a nerve by illustrating a "common and well intentioned mistake" of stretching a word out. How many of these examples have you seen your lawyers write?

definite	becomes	definitive
determine	becomes	determinate
life	becomes	lifespan
method	becomes	methodology
practical	becomes	practicable
simple	becomes	simplistic
use	becomes	utilize

We've seen them all. We haven't even questioned them, have we? What is added by this stretching out? Nothing.

Professor Pinckert also has a few words to say about jargon: "A good writer never touches it." He talks about jargon being used in technical writing—which legal writing is—and says: "The trouble with technical sounding terms is that they aren't technical: plain English is more precise. The trick in technical writing is to use plain language."

He says that if you "clarify the idea," the special word won't be needed, and asks that we "rethink the whole sentence or paragraph if you have to."

Profesor Pinckert praises brevity, "a rare and thrilling quality in writing," that "marks the distinguished mind." Our legal writing needs great infusions of brevity, which only result from hard work, clear *thinking*, and careful editing.

Writer's Digest, the successful and, many believe, foremost periodical for writers, published a compilation of some of its best articles to celebrate that magazine's 75th birthday in 1994.[10] I want to share the highlights of some of those articles over those 75 years.

W. Adolphe Roberts wrote in 1921 that one of the reasons he rejected 10,000 manuscripts was that they were "sloppily written."[11]

Louis Dodge, 1924, advised: "Say something," adding that if a paragraph or sentence were found to say nothing, he would "take it out relentlessly, no matter how pretty it may sound to the ear or how much distinction it may show to the eye. It is an intruder, it is an assassin which destroys the reader's interest and the writer's purpose."[12]

In 1931, Albert Payson Terhune advised that we "Write With Simplicity."[13]

Don James suggested in 1969: "Keep It Brief and Blend It In."[14]

Finally, Gary Provost, in a timeless 1984 article entitled "The Seven Beacons of Excellent Writing,"[15] lists *brevity* as the first, *clarity* as the second, and *precision* as the third on his useful list full of wisdom.

Brevity

Clarity

Precision

Let's remember those three words, if nothing else. They can be our beacons as we assist lawyers with their legal writing.

I cannot end this chapter without mentioning Gertrude Block. She is one of the best writing teachers and scholars in this country, with many books and columns to her credit. Gertrude Block is a modern-day master of grammatical matters. While she is not a plain language advocate, she *is* a proponent of precision and clarity. She is an authority on all forms of written communications. You can settle many an argument by referring to Ms. Block, so add her work to your reference library.

Nor can I fail to mention the fine little book, *Plain English for Lawyers*, written many years ago by Richard Wydick. It has endured and can be found in many law school book stores.

Now, with all that insightful advice from respected sources from in and out of the legal field, I rest my case. I hope you are gearing up to pare the legalese from your writing. You can start by editing others' work in some of your files, just for practice. See Appendix B for an editing checklist for guidance. You will find many wasted words every day in legal writing. Are you ready to start improving your own writing?

Examples of Improvement

The following examples of improvement over bad style have appeared thousands of times in pleadings and correspondence files of cases I've worked on. I'm sure you have seen them, too, and can think of more.

NOT	BETTER
advise us of your plans	notify us of your plans
the aforementioned section	the section on page 4
the aforesaid facts	the facts in paragraph 2
as per your request	as requested
at the time of his cashing of the check	when he cashed the check
by and through his undersigned attorney	by his attorney
a check in the sum of	a check for
do not hesitate to contact me	please call
enclosed herewith please find	enclosed is
in close proximity to	near
in the course of the trial	during the trial
in the event that	if
in line with your suggestion	as you suggested
it may be that	perhaps
may or may not	may
please accept my thanks	thank you

postpone until later	postpone
pursuant to our conversation	as we discussed
reach a decision	decide
under separate cover	separately
the undersigned represents X	I represent X
we carried out an analysis	we analyzed
we place the blame on Jones	we blame Jones
with reference to	concerning

Make some notes for yourself of some of these often-seen phrases that need to be streamlined or eliminated. You will see them every day in documents that either originate in your office or come to your office from other lawyers and businesses.

Soon we can get to some specifics, but first we should look at some of the rules that govern the technical side of our legal writing.

Endnotes

1. William Strunk Jr. and E. B. White, *The Elements of Style*, 3d ed. (New York, MacMillan Publishing Co., 1979).

2. Jan Vanolia, *Wright Right!* (Berkely, Ten Speed Press, 1988).

3. William Brohaugh, *Write Tight* (Cincinnati, Writer's Digest Books, 1993).

4. Rudolf Flesch, *How to Write, Speak and Think More Effectively—Your Complete Course in the Art of Communication* (New York: Printer's Ink Publishing Corp., 1946; 1951 compilation by Signet Books, div. of Harper Collins Publishers, Inc.), at 86.

5. *Id.* at 39.

6. *Id.* at 321.

7. Richard Lauchman, *Plain Style*, (New York, AMACOM, division of American Management Association, 1993).

8. Mary A. DeVries, *Internationally Yours* (Boston, Houghton Mifflin Co., 1994).

9. Robert C. Pinckert, *The Truth About English* (Englewood Cliffs, Prentice Hall, Inc., 1981.)

10. Editors of Writer's Digest, *The Writer's Digest Guide to Good Writing* (Cincinnati, Writer's Digest Books, 1994).

11. *Id.* at 4.

12. *Id.* at 15.

13. *Id.* at 38.

14. *Id.* at 198

15. *Id.* at 266-75.

CHAPTER 5

Rules We Must Follow

What Do the Rules Really Say?

If you haven't learned it yet, learn it now: you need authority for everything you do. If it's a grammar rule, your authority is the latest edition of the *Gregg Reference Manual*.[1] It's complete, easy to use, has an excellent index, and answers all questions. Some attorneys follow the *Chicago Manual of Style*.[2] If it's a citation rule, your authority is either *A Uniform System of Citation* ("The Bluebook")[3] or *The Chicago Manual of Legal Style* ("The Maroon Book"). The Bluebook is winning the race (much as VHS won over Beta), but the Maroon Book, with its signature lack of punctuation, is gathering increased fans in legal circles. Whichever authority you use, *use* it, and be consistent.

For pleadings and other matters involving court procedure, your authorities are the Rules of Procedure (civil, criminal, appellate, and evidence), both federal and those for your state.

Grammatical Rules

I'll say it again, strongly: If you don't have the latest version of the *Gregg Reference Manual* on your desk, get one. Now. It's your bible. It's your argument-settler. It's your authority. I want to cover a very few rules just to show that there are rules, authorities, and argument-settlers. You need know only where to look them up. In this section I refer to Gregg rules by section number for easy reference.

We find many self-perpetuating errors in legal documents. We make some of these errors because we see them in newspapers and magazines. Journalists with their space and time requirements have different rules and a wider latitude.

In 25 years of assisting lawyers, I've worked with several who write excellent briefs. Their thinking is organized and they write powerfully, but they have nothing but trouble with commas. Some want to just sprinkle them around, like salt. They think it just "must be time for a comma or two." They bring me the brief and say, "Fix the commas." (There are generally some other things to "fix," too.)

Two glaring examples of frequent punctuation errors are the commas that separate (most often before a conjunction in a series of three or more) and the commas that set off.

Commas that separate (*Gregg*, 123, 162-75):

a. **Items in a series require a comma before the conjunction.** Bryan Garner calls this the "serial comma" and it's his *first* punctuation rule in *The Elements of Legal Style*. His reason is succinct: "omitting it may cause ambiguities" but "including it never will." This rule is violated so often, I think, because we see it violated so often in the print media. Remember the comma before the conjunction in a series of three or more, and separate yourself from those who don't bother to learn the rules. Examples:

    Planes, trains, and automobiles

    Heart, mind, and body

Ordinances, statutes, and rules

John, Bill, and Sam

b. **A compound sentence requires a comma before the conjunction to separate the two main clauses:**

We can't go, but we think you should.

Janie did her homework, and then she washed the dishes.

We could take in a movie, or we could go boating.

Note that *each* of the clauses has a subject; the comma is not used when the clauses *share* a subject:

Janie did her homework and then washed the dishes.

Commas that set off (two commas) (*Gregg,* 122, 154-61):

a. **Dates: Commas before and after the year when it follows month and day. Do not use a comma between month and year with no day.**

On September 25, 1994, we had 14 inches of rain.

Joe's birthdate is December 1, 1964, and Jean's is July 4, 1968.

Note: see the "Trends" section at the end of this chapter.

We closed our practice at the end of May 1987.

b. **Jr., Sr., II, III, Esq.: Do not use a comma before unless you know the person prefers it.**

Gene Williams Jr. is on the board of directors.

IF a comma is used before, another is used after:

John Smith, Jr., will speak at the luncheon.

Abbreviations for Esquire, academic degrees, and religious titles are set off by two commas when they follow a name:

Send the letter to George Washington, Esq., in New York.

Kenton Whitsett, J.D., will substitute for Mr. Norman.

The Reverend Lawrence Jackson, S.J., will meet with us on Tuesday.

c.   **With Inc. and Ltd.:** This rule is just like the one for Jr. and Sr.: **Do not use a comma before unless you know the company prefers it.**

Johnson Roofing Inc. (Look at their letterhead or ask.)

IF a comma is used before, another is used after:

Jetero Publishing, Inc., is having a clearance sale.

Exception: drop the second comma after a possessive ending.

Jetero Publishing, Inc.'s board meets the third Tuesday.

Plurals and Possessives (*Gregg*, 601-51)

a.   **Pluralize first, then make it possessive:**

Men's (of more than one man)
Horses' (of more than one horse)
Ladies' (of more than one lady)

The Perkinses' house (belonging to more than one person named Perkins)

If the singular ends in an s, be guided by pronunciation. Add 's if the *pronunciation* adds a syllable; otherwise, add apostrophe only:

the witness's answer
Mr. Morris's briefcase
Mr. Reynolds' speech
New Orleans' cajun food

Pluralize the main noun in compound terms:

Attorneys general
Notaries public
Senators-elect
Passersby
Letters of absence

(Sadly, the repeated misuse of some of these terms has resulted in standards being lowered to accommodate custom. Now it is *accepted* to use "notary publics," "attorney generals," and "court-martials," but not *preferred*. The better practice is to use the preferred form, period.)

Don't confuse possessives with contractions (*Gregg*, 1063):

"Who's coming for dinner?"
"Whose car was responsible for the accident?"

Numbers

Gregg devotes the entire fourth chapter to numbers. You must study the chapter to become familiar with all the rules, as they are quite complicated. I will mention a few of the basics here, because you will always have numbers in pleadings.

The first distinction that needs to be made is that there are two *styles* to consider: the figure style and the word style. Since the figure style is the simplest and plainest, I use it except where good reason dictates or style needs to prevail.

Spell out numbers from 1 through 10; use figures for numbers above 10 (*Gregg*, 401), but if any number in a related group is over 10, use figures for all in the group (*Gregg*, 402):

Jones was doing 50 in a 10-mile zone.

Miller's facial injuries called for four stitches.

The cargo includes 98 crates of beans, but only 6 crates of onions.

Spell out a numbers above 10 at the beginning of a sentence, for ordinals and fractions, and for minimizing importance (*Gregg*, 401):

Three hundred persons is the room's capacity.

They celebrated their fiftieth anniversary.

Amalgamated lost one-fourth of its revenue.

I thought of thousands of reasons not to go.

For numbers in the millions (*Gregg*, 403):

25 million (*not* 25,000,000)

1.5 billion (*not* 1,500,000,000)

but: 5,867,932

Money:

$10 million (*Gregg,* 413-20)

If the lawyer insists on writing money in words and figures, refer to *Gregg,* 420, and at least do it correctly:

Two Thousand Dollars ($2,000)
—*not* Two Thousand ($2,000) Dollars

Do not add decimal point and zeroes to whole dollar amounts in a sentence (*Gregg,* 415).

I enclose my $250 check
—*not* I enclose my $250.00 check

Abbreviations (*Gregg,* chapter 5):

Always choose the shortest (*Gregg,* 502):

2d, not 2nd
3d, not 3rd

Don't use periods when unnecessary (*Gregg,* 520, 522, 524):

GAO, IRS, NYSE, OSHA, ESOP

Never abbreviate "Fort," "Mount," "Point," or "Port," but always abbreviate "Saint" in place names (*Gregg* 529):

Fort Worth
Mount Holyoke
St. Louis

That or which (*Gregg* 1062):

Lawyers are notorious for not getting these right.

As a basic rule, **use "that" to introduce a phrase that is *essential* to the meaning of the sentence and "which" to introduce a phrase that is merely additional material.**

The flying debris that hit Jones caused serious injuries.

(Not the debris from the hurricane or the debris on the floor, but this particular debris—the debris that hit Jones.

It's essential to determine which debris, so it's introduced by "that.")

Thompson's brief, which was filed October 15, was neither timely nor on point. (*Additional material, not essential.*)

That or who (*Gregg* 1062):

"Who" refers to an individual person; "that" may be used to refer to a class or species.

It was Richardson *who* ran the light.

It is industries *that* pollute the environment *that* should be punished by these statutes.

There are times when these rules do not apply, so be sure to review section 1062 of *Gregg* entirely for answers to all questions about *that, which, and who*. It's pretty complicated and definitely not for the timid or lazy.

If you make friends with your reference books, you will never regret it.

To Hyphenate or Not?

In general, **do not hyphenate prefixes** (*Gregg* 833-41), but always consider clarity.

This is another area where legal writers seem to think that a sprinkling is necessary, and they're nearly always wrong.

Pre, post, anti, and most other prefixes are generally *not* hyphenated:

pretrial
cosigner
extralegal
proactive
multipurpose
midstream
fourfold
semiannual
reelect

but: chicken coop, farmers' co-op, post-trial

Most "non" words are not hyphenated. Check any current edition of Webster's and you will find a thorough (but not exhaustive—the better the dictionary, the more complete) list of words beginning with "non" that are no longer hyphenated.

nonsuit
nonallergic
nonnegotiable
noneffective
noneduational
nonsupporting
nonverbal
nontransferable

but: non-interest-bearing

How many of these surprised you? Take a look at *Gregg* and your eyes will be opened. Take a good look at any dictionary and you'll find many more.

Errors in Legal Terminology

These errors are self-perpetuating. They can be caused by laziness (the LA doesn't look the term up) or lack of knowledge. You should never be far from a legal dictionary. It should never be "too much trouble" to look up a word you're unsure of. For example:

Parol evidence—*not parole evidence*—is extrinsic evidence.

Express—*not* express*ed*—or implied authority is an issue found in agency law.

Therefor and wherefor, although not plain language words, are completely different words, with different meanings, from *therefore and wherefore*. If you *must* use them, at least use them correctly.

"Therefor" means "for that": *in payment therefor* (not *therefore*)

"Therefore" means logically following: *I think; therefore, I am.*

The subject of legal terminology brings me to one of our specialties in the legal field: briefs and legal memoranda. Again, your authority is the latest edition of the Harvard Bluebook. The latest edition (the 15th) is much more user friendly than past other edition. Every LA should know this book from cover to cover to be able to find things quickly. The only way to be that familiar with it is to spend some time with it. Make friends with it. Here are some common problem, with references to the rule numbers.

Common Errors in
Appellate Briefs and Legal Memoranda

Some legal writers just type whatever happens to "look nice," I suppose, never dreaming that there might be particular rules governing things such as spacing in abbreviations. The rule is: Always space *before* and *after* an abbreviation of more than one letter; individual numbers, whether numerals or ordinals, are treated as single capitals (6.1(e)). Learning this one rule will save you many look-ups.

F.2d
S.W.2d
So. 2d
S. Ct.
Fed. R. Civ. P.
Fed. Supp.
F.R.D.

Always cite to the *official* code or reporter (12.2.1).

An annotated version is not official. The official federal code is the United States Code (U.S.C.). United States Code Annotated (U.S.C.A.) is an *unofficial* federal code.

For the United States Supreme Court, the official reporter is United States Reports, abbreviated "U.S." The Bluebook tells us to not give a parallel citation (Table T.1). But the official reporter lags far behind the private companies in publishing opinions. Also, a particular court (such as the Fifth Circuit, for many years) may have only the Lawyers Edition, instead of the Supreme Court Reporter. We are therefore forced by particular circumstances to give parallel citations at times:

Smith v. Jones, ___ U.S. ___, 103 S. Ct. 1356, 16 L. Ed. 2d 840 (19xx).

Omissions in quoted matter (5.3):

An ellipsis indicates that words have been omitted from a quoted passage. It is three *spaced* periods. At the end of a sentence, it's four spaced periods.

> A defendant whose property . . . has been garnished .   . may
> . . . seek to vacate . . . .

Alterations in quoted matter (5.2):

Enclose a *changed* letter or a *substitution* in brackets. This happens when you, as the author, need to make changes to the material you are quoting.

For example, you may pick from the middle of a quote, but it begins the sentence in your work, so it requires a capital letter. You also may need to insert an explanatory word to a quoted passage.

> "[P]ublic confidence in the [adversary] system depends upon full disclosure."

Under the same rule, it is noted that indication of any change of emphasis or omission of citations is to be in *parentheses*.

(Don't ask me why!)

NEVER begin a quotation with an ellipsis (5.3b):

Use an ellipsis when omitting language from the middle of a quote. If the omission is at the end of a quoted sentence, the fourth spaced period is the ending punctuation.

Block indented quotations (5.1):

> Quotations of more than 50 words do not have quotation marks and
> are block indented (left and right). The block indenting indicates that
> it's a quotation. Since you do not use quotation marks to indicate this
> quoted matter, an internal quote appearing within that quotation,
> requires regular double quotation marks.

> Quotations of fewer than 50 words are included in the narrative text,
> and internal quotations use single quotation marks: "The court of
> appeals noted the 'long hair rule' adopted by the school district."

> Do not use symbols or citation abbreviations in the narrative portions
> of a brief. Use symbols and abbreviations in citations only.

> Spell out "section" and "paragraph" in text, except when referring
> to the U.S. Code or a federal regulation.

> Symbols may be used in citations and footnotes. If symbols are used,
> include a space between the symbol and the numeral. (6.2b.)

Court Procedural Rules

Any LA who works in litigation knows that there are rules of
procedure governing all litigation, in every court. We know where to
look up the rules. We know we must live by them.

Rule 8, Federal Rules of Civil Procedure, is titled "General Rules of
Pleading." It says that a pleading shall contain a *short and plain
statement* of jurisdictional grounds, a *short and plain statement* of the
claim showing that pleader is entitled to relief, and a demand for
judgment. Under subdivision (e) of that same rule we find: "Each
averment of a pleading shall be simple, concise, and direct." I have
expanded the discussion of pleading format in chapter 7.

Rule 10, Federal Rules of Civil Procedure, sets forth the
requirements for pleadings. It says that every pleading shall contain a
caption setting forth the name of the court, the title of the action, the file
number, and a designation as in Rule 7(a) [pleadings allowed]. Rule 10
then says that all averments of claim or defense shall be made in
numbered paragraphs, limited to a single set of circumstances.

Now, that's a pleading, per the federal rules. Say it directly, concisely, with no verbosity or senseless drivel. We need to know quickly: What is the claim? Many hours will be spent in discovery finding out the details. Our initial pleading should put the defendant on notice of what it is we claim he's done, and what we want to be made whole. Defendant's initial pleading should clearly respond to each allegation and state why he isn't liable or shouldn't have to pay.

Conciseness and clarity should be the major thrust of your legal documents. I will refer to all court documents as "pleadings." Until very recent times, motions have not been considered "pleadings." Real "pleadings" are things like the complaint or petition (or whatever latest amendment), the answer of defendant, same for any third parties, and generally, any document which states the position in the lawsuit of a particular party. Neither motions nor discovery matters are considered "pleadings."

As a matter of practice, however, lawyers have come to put all documents filed in a lawsuit into files marked "Pleadings," and to refer to all of them as "pleadings." Some court rules even state now that motions shall be considered pleadings. It is well known that trends become the norm (just as plain language will do some day), so it's just a matter of time before the archaic "motions are not *pleadings*" will fall by the wayside. I will, for the sake of clarity, refer to all documents filed in a lawsuit as "pleadings."

Trends Bucking the Rules

Plain language is the way we talk. That means split infinitives, dangling prepositions, and pronouns not agreeing with their antecedents. These are seen as violations by grammatical scholars but are accepted by the plain language movement as well as modern thinkers. Again, this is the way we talk. These are trends we should be aware of (formerly, *of which we should be aware*).

Split Infinitives:

"to boldly go where no man has gone"
"failed to timely perfect an appeal"

Dangling prepositions:

"What have I gotten myself into?"
"What did he hit her with?"

Pronoun not agreeing with antecedent:

"The CCS goal is to get the consumer back on *their* feet."

Old formatting rules are being questioned, now that we have professional-quality fonts on our computers. For instance, it is now considered archaic to space twice after a period. It's just no longer needed. We who learned to type on a typewriter find it necessary to unlearn some things now that we have computers.

It's also no longer necessary to use two hyphens to type a dash, since we have the capability to make an em dash, not available on a typewriter. And even the rule about commas that set off, used with dates and city-state combinations, is being cast aside.

If you are a competent professional, you will be aware of and observe major trends. We can never be complacent in our knowledge but must instead always be *aware* of changes.

As you begin to look for ways to make your (or your lawyer's) writing more concise, you will find opportunities in every paragraph. And you will become good at it very quickly. It just takes practice.

Endnotes

1. William A. Sabin, *The Gregg Reference Manual*, 7th ed. (New York, Macmillan-McGraw Hill, Glencoe Division, 1993).

2. *The Chicago Manual of Style*, 14th ed., and *The Chicago Manual of Legal Style* (Chicago, University of Chicago Press, 1993).

3. *The Bluebook, A Uniform System of Citation*, 15th ed. (Cambridge, The Harvard Law Review Association, 1991).

CHAPTER 6

Analysis of a Pleading

The Parts of a Pleading

If you analyze a pleading, you will understand *why* things are done, rather than blindly follow forms which might perpetuate errors handed down from generation to generation in a law office.

The parts of a pleading are:

1. Caption

2. Title of the Document

3. Body of the Document

4. Prayer

5. Signature Block

6. Endorsement (if necessary, e.g., Jury Demand)

7. Certificate of Conference (if required)

8. Verification (if required)

9. Certificate of Service

Several Forms of a Caption

We generally defer to the custom of our area with regard to form. There may be local rules requiring certain formats to be used. Is there a *reason* that pleadings in your cases in your area are in a certain form? Is it custom? Is it the signing lawyer's preference? California and Colorado require all pleadings to be on lined paper. Follow your local rules; you can get a copy at the clerk's office.

The forms in the Appendix of Forms at the end of the Federal Rules of Civil Procedure give examples from the Southern District of New York, with the file number at the top and the title of the document on the right side. I've already told you that since I'm from Texas, most of these forms will be as used in Texas. Look at the pleadings in your office. Even better, go to the file room of any court and look at some of the pleadings filed there. You can check out files or look at documents on microfiche or other storage media. The records are open to the public.

For example, California requires attorney identification and representative capacity in the upper left corner of pleadings. Some courts require paper with numbered lines, 25 to a page. I would be willing to bet, however, that even if you used a Texas form in a California court, it would be filed.

The caption contains the most requested piece of information in any lawsuit: the case number, frequently called the cause number. You will be asked for it every time you call or visit a clerk's office. Never call a clerk for information on a case without having the case number. After retrieving the file by the case number, the clerk will then verify the parties to confirm that you are both talking about the same case.

The caption, signature block, and certificate of service are used on every pleading, so you will want to have them in your pleading shell document for each case.

Caption
(Using Closed Punctuation)

(1)   IN THE UNITED STATES DISTRICT COURT
                SOUTHERN DISTRICT OF TEXAS
                      HOUSTON DIVISION

(2) JOHN SMITH, a minor, by	§	
Next Friend MARCIA SMITH,	§	
and MARCIA SMITH,	§	
Individually,	§	
	§	
Plaintiffs,	§	(3) CIVIL ACTION NO.
	§	
v.	§	_____
	§	
EVIL TRUCKING CO.,	§	(4) JURY
a corporation, and	§	
RICHARD BADD,	§	
	§	
Defendants.	§	

The caption identifies the court (1), the parties and their designations (2), and the cause number (3). Local rules often require that the caption indicate, on every pleading, whether a jury has been demanded (4). The cause number and perhaps the particular court division will be blank until assigned after filing.

Some forms of state court pleadings have the cause number centered at the top and the court on the right-hand side. Follow the rules and sample forms for your state or federal district. Notice that the caption shown above uses *closed punctuation*, with the parts separated by commas, a period after the "v.," and a period at the end. Some use a section symbol, as I have, and some use a right parenthesis as separation. Follow the custom in your area.

Speaking of the "versus," how many ways can it be typed? If the abbreviation is used, one would expect it to be followed by a period, and I will do so in this book. However, everybody—but everybody—knows what the "versus" means. I have seen it all of the following ways: V, V., v, v., -v-, -V-, -vs-, -VS-, -vs.-, versus, VERSUS, and probably several others. If it makes sense, do it.

Caption
(Using Partially Closed Punctuation)

IN THE UNITED STATES DISTRICT COURT
SOUTHERN DISTRICT OF TEXAS
HOUSTON DIVISION

JOHN SMITH, a minor, by	§	
Next Friend MARCIA SMITH,	§	
and MARCIA SMITH,	§	
Individually,	§	
	§	
Plaintiffs	§	CIVIL ACTION NO.
	§	
v.	§	_____
	§	
EVIL TRUCKING CO.,	§	(4) JURY
a corporation, and	§	
RICHARD BADD,	§	
	§	
Defendants	§	

Partially closed punctuation is most commonly used, where a comma follows the name of the plaintiff and that of the defendant.

Punctuation is not required, however, and many lawyers and judges prefer no punctuation, called *open punctuation*, in the caption. If the party designations are offset, there is no question about who is plaintiff and who is defendant. The cleaner look, and the format which I will use in this book, is open punctuation, as seen in the next example.

Caption
(Using Open Punctuation)

IN THE UNITED STATES DISTRICT COURT
SOUTHERN DISTRICT OF TEXAS
HOUSTON DIVISION

JOHN SMITH, a minor, by	§	
Next Friend MARCIA SMITH	§	
and MARCIA SMITH,	§	
Individually	§	
	§	
Plaintiffs	§	CIVIL ACTION NO.
	§	
v.	§	_____
	§	
EVIL TRUCKING CO.,	§	(4) JURY
a corporation, and	§	
RICHARD BADD	§	
	§	
Defendants	§	

I think this open punctuation looks cleaner, uncluttered. Defer to your attorney's choice if you can't convince him otherwise. Don't worry about a little skirmish. Try to win the war.

It is only the *initial* pleading on behalf of a party which requires full information on the parties. Lawsuits with numerous parties give birth to captions that run for over a page. It is necessary to list *all* parties only when we amend to add or delete.

Subsequent pleadings in cases where the parties do not change require only the first-named party in each category. Subsequent pleadings in the example case would be abbreviated as:

Caption
(Abbreviated)

IN THE UNITED STATES DISTRICT COURT
SOUTHERN DISTRICT OF TEXAS
HOUSTON DIVISION

JOHN SMITH, etc., et al.	§	
	§	
Plaintiffs	§	CIVIL ACTION NO.
	§	
v.	§	_____
	§	
EVIL TRUCKING CO., et al.	§	(4) JURY
	§	
Defendants	§	

Notice two things about this abbreviated caption:

1. The "etc." stands for the information about this little boy named John Smith, bringing the action through his mother and next friend, as required by the rules of procedure for this minor to have *standing* in the court. Everybody in this lawsuit knows after they read the complaint that John Smith is a minor and is bringing the action through his next friend, as required by law. Why repeat it in every pleading? It's not wrong if you do, but you can save expensive printer and copier toner by omitting it. (Could you also use an "etc." after the first-named defendant, to indicate the corporation? Probably. Is it required or necessary? Probably not.)

2. The "et al." stands for a Latin phrase, *et alia*, meaning "and others." Therefore, when we abbreviate that Latin phrase, a period is

required after the "1." Omitting that period is a common error, even among experienced LAs.

As to the jury demand, it is enough to write "Jury," but local rules may require "Jury Demanded" or other particular words. Again, check the rules for the court in which you are filing.

3. Do you really need to add "plaintiff" and "defendant" in subsequent pleadings? No. It is obvious who the parties are, so plain language principles dictate that you omit the party designations in subsequent pleadings.

Title of Document

If space permits, triple-space on either side of the title of the document. This is an aesthetic, artistic consideration only; there are no rules dictating triple-spacing before and after the title. It's purely a matter of preference. Space is a more important consideration. If triple-spacing makes a two-page document go to three pages, by all means, don't do it.

Make the title of the document as short as possible. But if the title is more than one line, single space it and underline only the bottom line, making that one underline as long as the longest line in the title. If a title is double-spaced, it's okay to underline each line, but do not underline each line when single-spaced. I have seen some pleadings with titles four to six lines long. Is that really necessary? No. To make matters worse, every line was underlined. It looked cluttered, at the least.

Judge Hughes tells us to "make the label useful." For example, "Motion for Summary Judgment" is nice and short, but doesn't tell us as much as we need to know. "Johnson's Motion for Judgment on Limitations" is admittedly longer, but much more precise and therefore helpful to the judge or whoever reads it.

How about this one?

COLUMBIA BANKING & TRUST COMPANY OF DELAWARE, INC.'S MOTION TO DISQUALIFY ATTORNEYS FOR THE THIRD-PARTY DEFENDANT THOMAS H. DENTON OR IN THE ALTERNATIVE FOR SANCTIONS

This, says Judge Hughes, is "positively sick!" It is not required, anywhere that I can find, that the title of a document contain everything you're asking for. You can ask for sanctions in the document itself without having to include them in the title of the document. This title can be shortened from 26 to 6 words.

A much better title for this document would be:

COLUMBIA'S MOTION TO DISQUALIFY DENTON'S COUNSEL

As to underlining, I say keep it to a minimum. Bolding, without underlining, looks clean and crisp, compared to underlining. If your document has many levels of subheadings, you may have to combine bolding with underlining to differentiate among the levels, such as:

TITLE OF DOCUMENT

NEXT LEVEL

Next Level

Next Level

Final Level

If your computer will easily convert to italics for case names or emphasis, without a complete font change, choose italics over underlining. It's much easier to read and looks more professional.

Body of Document

The body of the pleading contains information about the parties, jurisdiction (and maybe venue) allegations, the allegations about the claim or defense, and the damages claimed.

The federal rules require numbered paragraphs, and that means arabic numbers, not roman numerals. There is no rule of which I am aware that requires roman numeral outline format for pleadings. Using consecutive arabic numbers is the best practice and the easiest to follow. It is often helpful to add titles to sections of the pleading, such as "Jurisdiction and Venue," "Background," "Conspiracy," "Fraud," "Affirmative Defenses," and the like. But those titles are for convenience of reference for the reader and organization for the writer and do not need any kind of identifying number.

Do Not Use: "May It Please the Court" or "To the Honorable Judge of Said Court" or other useless formalism to introduce the body of the document. It serves no purpose, doesn't impress anyone, and you won't be penalized for omitting it.

Structure: In structuring your sentences, put power in the first part, with a strong verb. Lawyers are famous for stringing together phrases at the beginning of a sentence as introductory material, and we don't find their positive statement until the end. The result is lost power.

I've tried to figure out why lawyers do this. I think it must be to thwart arguments against the statements they are making. A lawyer's mind is analytical; a good lawyer always anticipates defenses. This weakens our writing.

Example: "In view of the language quoted in the case of *Circle K Ranch v. XXX Insurance Company*, except for the issue of misrepresentations, defendants' topics of discovery are irrelevant. Texas law is clear . . . ."

See how all those introductory phrases weaken the sentence? The reader must search diligently, and even go back and read it again, to find the meaning. How much more powerful it is to begin the sentence with: "Defendant's discovery topics are irrelevant."

Separate Counts: Rule 8(e) of the Federal Rules of Civil Procedure permits claims to be set forth in separate statements or counts.

Example:

1. Count One, claim for damages for negligence

2. Count Two, loss of consortium

3. Count Three, exemplary or punitive damages

In each case, paragraphs containing the allegations common to each, such as the circumstances surrounding the event made the basis of the suit, will be adopted by reference in the other counts.

Example:

Count Two
Loss of Consortium

16. Jones adopts by reference the allegations of paragraphs 1 through 15.

With multiple counts, you do not adopt *everything* th: gone before. You adopt the paragraphs containing the facts needed   .ay the predicate. The better practice, then, is to lay out all the factual allegations in preliminary paragraphs—in the above case, the first 15 paragraphs—and then adopt paragraphs 1 through 15 at the start of each new count.

Considerations for the Body of the Pleading

What About Capitalization?

If it's not a proper noun, if it isn't in a title, and if it doesn't begin a sentence or a line, don't capitalize it. In the body of a pleading, "plaintiff" and "defendant" are not proper nouns. Titles of documents, such as "complaint," "answer," "motion for summary judgment," or "final judgment" are not proper nouns. "Bill of sale," "contract," and "warranty deed" are not proper nouns. *They should not be capitalized.* And as for the practice of typing names of parties in *all capitals?* Absolutely not. What can be the reason which would override the fact that it detracts from the content of the document? Yet disputes linger over capitalization because our authorities are not in agreement.

The Bluebook advises us in the Practitioners' Notes, P.6 at page 17, to follow rule 8 concerning capitalization. The Harvard people *also* tell us to capitalize party designations when referring to parties in the subject litigation, listing as examples "Plaintiff" and "Appellant." But the trend is *away* from capitalization. Plain language proponents such as Judge Hughes tell us *not* to capitalize party designations. I agree. It probably is a matter of deference or a sign of showing respect. But is it necessary? No. When in doubt, honor trends.

The Bluebook also tells us to capitalize "court" when referring to the court that will be receiving the document—which would be the judge or panel in the subject litigation. Of course, we also follow rule 8, which is to capitalize "court" when naming any court in full or when referring to the United States Supreme Court. The practice of capitalizing "court" when referring to the court you are addressing is a good one, and indicates respect, so I believe it is a good practice. "Court" rises to a different level than does "plaintiff" or "defendant."

When in doubt, do not capitalize. Go with the trend, which is *away* from capitalization. It reads much better and flows more smoothly without unnecessary, distracting capital letters.

What About Numbers?

In the "olden days," it was fashionable always to write numbers in words and figures. It is another senseless custom. I have even seen it done in letters—an abominable practice. Has it continued because we use words and figures on checks? If there is a dispute as to a check amount, the spelled-out wording will control. In financial documents, such as a bill of sale, words and figures are acceptable and perhaps necessary. In a document concerning quantities, it is probably also acceptable and perhaps necessary. But in a pleading or a letter? No. Use figures only.

I recently received a letter from a lawyer enclosing tickets to a Houston Rockets basketball game. The letter began with:

Enclosed herewith are two (2) tickets.

What was the purpose of that? And why didn't the lawyer catch it and correct it? This was a nice, friendly letter. Whenever I read something like that, I can only assume an inexperienced secretary (or lawyer doing his own typing) has just learned about words and figures and uses it everywhere, just to be sure. The lawyer is so accustomed to seeing it, he doesn't question it. It demonstrates a lack of thinking.

Which of the following is easier to read and understand?

1.   Plaintiff's contract called for payment of Four Hundred Seventy-Five Thousand Dollars ($475,000.00) on the first (1st) day of April and October.

2.   Jones agreed to pay Smith $475,000 on April 1 and October 1.

The answer is obvious. The second sentence is much easier. The attention flows to the content, and the content is understood. We have real *communication*.

Compare it to the extra mental processes required to read and understand the first sentence. First of all, our attention stops for a nanosecond or millisecond to remember who "Plaintiff" is. Then we have to slow down to read the spelled-out number. Then we get hung up by the ".00" at the end of the parenthetical figures, trying to decide how many zeroes there are, and if the figures match the words.

The zeroes brings up another point. The *Gregg Reference Manual* will be your best friend when it comes to numbers. Two rule violations frequently found in pleadings involve zeroes.

1. Do not use .00 when referring to whole dollars in a sentence. (Gregg, 415.) Say: *Smith's medical bills total $8,345.* Or: *Jones paid $15,600 on the contract.* Forget the extra zeroes.

2. Do not use figures for round amounts of a million or more. (Gregg, 416.) Say: *Jones seeks judgment of $12 million.* Or *$12.5 million* for $12,500,000 or *$12.4 million* for $12,400,000. If, however, the amount is a more complicated figure, such as *12,465,770*, use all figures (but never words as well).

What About Citations?

You use legal citations in your arguments in support of motions as well as in appellate briefs. What are some of the most violated rules? What will help us? See chapter 5 of this book for helpful hints and see the Bluebook or the Maroon Book for details.

There are two glaring errors that are exceedingly common. One is the wrong abbreviation, period. The other is in using citations within a narrative. I'll give you an example of each.

Using the Wrong Abbreviation:

In their notes, many lawyers abbreviate abbreviations. Whoever types it, picks it up; it is repeated, and finally it becomes custom (again). But it's not correct. For example, the Federal Rules of Civil Procedure are abbreviated *Fed. R. Civ. P.*—not F.R.C.P. and not FRCP. Unless you know the correct abbreviation, look it up. And remember, with all citations, abbreviations of more than one letter have a space before and after.

Using Abbreviations and Symbols in Narrative:

Abbreviations and symbols belong in citations—not sentences. In sentences you write out, fully, "Federal Rules of Civil Procedure" as well as "section" and "paragraph." It is correct to use abbreviations and symbols only in citations, as opposed to narrative.

Correct: **Under Rule 11, Federal Rules of Civil Procedure, sanctions may be imposed.**

Also
correct: **The court may impose sanctions. Fed. R. Civ. P. 11.**

Wrong: **Under Rule 11, Fed. R. Civ. P., sanctions may be imposed.**

Correct: **In section (c) of Rule 10, Federal Rules of Civil Procedure, it is clear that a written instrument which is an exhibit to a pleading is part of the pleading for all purposes.**

Also
correct: **It is not necessary to adopt by reference a written instrument attached as an exhibit, because it is part of the pleading for all purposes. Fed. R. Civ. P. 10(c).**

Wrong: **In § (c) of Rule 10, Federal Rules of Civil Procedure, it is clear that a written instrument which is an exhibit to a pleading is part of the pleading for all purposes.**

Do you see the difference? It separates the professionals from the beginners.

Prayer

This has been the "Wherefore Premises Considered" part of the pleading, but *please* eliminate that phrase from your pleadings. It is enough to call it a "Claim" or a "Demand" and to say that "Plaintiffs claim damage and interest under the law." I'm sure the "wherefore" is not necessary.

Well, you may say, what about including "all such other and further relief, both general and special, legal and equitable, to which the plaintiffs may be deemed to be justly entitled"? Isn't all of that included in the word "damage"? Is it required that you include a catch-all phrase in the prayer, just in case?

There is a bugaboo among young lawyers, especially, that remains with them until they're grown-up, allegedly confident lawyers. That bugaboo is a fear that somebody will want to give them something they haven't asked for; they can't get it if they haven't asked for it, so they throw everything in—just in case. While I agree that there will be occasions where you must follow a statute verbatim, some things can be carried to the point of being ridiculous. This is one of them.

In Texas, case law almost makes our state a fact pleading state. I won't belabor this narrative with a lot of citations, but according to *Texas Jurisprudence (3d)*, the cases say that "[n]ot only must the relief granted a plaintiff have support in a specific or general prayer in his petition, but it is also elementary that in order to sustain a judgment, the relief asked, and granted by the judgment, must be consistent with the facts alleged."

Lawyers don't want to be in the position of not getting some relief because they didn't ask for it, but that's not really what would happen. I have discussed it with several Texas judges, and they all agree that if that happened, the party could amend his pleading to conform.

You may recall "The Verdict," a fine trial movie starring Paul Newman. It is about a medical malpractice case. The jury comes back and asks if they can give the plaintiffs more than they asked for. The judge answers "yes."

Actually, a plaintiff must allege enough facts in a petition that it is certain what he intends to prove at trial. A prayer for relief may not be inconsistent with the facts, nor will it be read as enlarging the petition to embrace a cause of action not pleaded. If a prayer for relief is to be construed, if there is an *intent* by the pleader to claim the relief granted, the judgment will be upheld.

We in Texas have a creature called "special exceptions," and the court may require the plaintiff to amend and make the pleading more specific. It's like the Rule 12 motion to make more definite and certain in federal court. That doesn't mean it can't be written clearly, though. Know the rules and case law in your state.

According to the Appendix of Forms in the federal rules, the prayer need say only:

Wherefore plaintiff demands judgment against defendant in the sum of $_____ and costs.

Of course, I question the "wherefore" and don't see that it's needed.

Signature Block

The signature block contains the name, address, telephone number, and fax number of the attorney filing the pleading. It should also contain some number identifying the lawyer. Some courts assign numbers and some use the state bar numbers. The federal court in Houston first assigned ID numbers to each lawyer admitted to practice in the district, then changed the policy and asked the lawyers to use their state bar ID numbers. Now most lawyers give both numbers.

Check the local rules to make sure you are doing it correctly. For instance, some rules require that only one attorney be a "designated attorney in charge" or something similar. Those rules might call for only that attorney's name and other information to be in the signature block, with firm names and names of other counsel working on the case off to the left. That rule has been the case in the Southern District of Texas for almost ten years, and we still have lawyers and law firms not conforming to it. Placement of the signature block may also be defined in the local rules.

Endorsement
(Jury Demand)

If a jury is demanded, it may be "endorsed" on the pleading. That amounts to nothing more than typing "Plaintiffs demand a jury." beneath the signature block. A jury also may be demanded in the body of the pleading. It can even be added as almost an afterthought:

Plaintiff demands judgment against defendant for $2 million, lawful interest and costs, and demands a trial by jury.

One important thing to remember about the jury demand, procedurally, is that it must be demanded within ten days of "the filing of the last pleading to the triable issue" or it is *waived*.

Certificate of Conference

If the rules in your jurisdiction don't call for a certificate of conference, it's only a matter of time until they do. Judges want to know that attorneys have tried to work things out between them before resorting to filing motions. Therefore, some local rules have specific provisions calling for attorneys to note in a certificate of conference that they have conferred with opposing counsel before filing the motion. Some rules require the attorney to list dates and modes of communication. Surprisingly, sometimes that one phone call will make filing the motion unnecessary. When working on a motion, call first; you might save some time. Again, check your local rules.

The certificate of conference is very simple:

I conferred with John Doe, counsel for XXX, by telephone on September 15, 19xx, who advised that the motion is opposed.

The attorney then signs it and is bound by the provisions of Rule 11.

Verification

Is your pleading one that requires verification, such as in a sworn account case? If so, it must be included. It simply verifies that the allegations in the pleading are within the signer's personal knowledge and are true. Verifications and affidavits are fertile ground for archaic formalisms. The "ss," which is a punishable offense on our Gobbledygook Fee Schedule, is an example. It is an abbreviation for the Latin word *scilicety*, meaning "more particularly" or (even worse) "to-wit." Get rid of it. You don't need it.

Here are forms for an individual and a corporate verification:

Individual verification:

STATE OF TENNESSEE   )
)
COUNTY OF HARDEMAN   )

John Smith states on his oath that he has read the foregoing [title of document], that the matters stated are within his personal knowledge and are true, except those matters stated to be upon information and belief,* and those he believes to be true.

_____ [date]

_____ [signature]

Sworn to and signed before me by John Smith on [date].

_____

[notary's signature and printed name]
[seal and date commission expires]

*[Check with your attorney: in some cases, "information and belief" is not enough; it must be on personal knowledge.]

Corporate verification:

STATE OF TENNESSEE   )
)
COUNTY OF HARDEMAN   )

John Smith states on his oath that he is the [office held] of [name of corporation], that he has read the foregoing [title of document], that the matters stated are within his personal knowledge and are true, except those matters stated to be upon information and belief, and those he believes to be true, and that he is authorized by the corporation to sign this verification as the act of the corporation.

_____ [date]

_____ [signature]

Sworn to and signed before me by John Smith on [date].

[seal]   _____
                          [notary's signature and printed name]

[seal and date commission expires]

I'm sure you noticed that these verifications may have some unnecessary words. Again, think. Are they really necessary? Does some statute require them? Is there a prescribed form without which your document won't be filed and you will lose the case? I seriously doubt it. You can still cut out some words.

The "information and belief" provision is a copout. It's another example of trying to cover every single possibility, of trying to anticipate every argument, of trying to be too thorough.

If the signer cannot swear to everything, if there are things that are borderline and may not be true of the signer's own personal knowledge, then don't include them. Simple enough, isn't it? But as always, check with your attorney.

Several years ago the State Bar of Texas cleaned up our real estate forms and the body of an acknowledgment now says only:

This instrument was acknowledged before me on [date] by [name].

Now, that's plain language.

Here is a plain language verification:

STATE OF TEXAS   §
                              §
COUNTY OF HARRIS   §

On this day J. Trent Hamilton appeared before me, and after I

administered the oath, he stated that the facts in this motion are within

his personal knowledge and are true.

_____

J. Trent Hamilton

Sworn to and signed before me by J. Trent Hamilton on [date].

_____

[seal]   Notary Public, State of Texas

I have seen jurats that saw "Sworn to and subscribed" and others
that say "Subscribed and sworn to." I was told by an attorney in a
seminar that "Subscribed and sworn to" was correct, but I didn't believe
it. I've always thought that "Sworn to and subscribed" had to be correct,
because the signer was sworn in before signing, then signed it in the
presence of the notary (differing from an acknowledgment, which may
already have been signed and the signer is merely acknowledging signing
it). Aside from the fact that "subscribed" should be changed to "signed,"
is it not correct to state that it was "sworn to" before it was signed?

Affidavit

Affidavits are necessary as evidence and are more detailed than
verifications. They are frequently attached to motions for summary
judgment and motions to compel discovery. In a 1994 case (*Humphreys
v. Caldwell*), the Supreme Court of Texas ruled an affidavit invalid

because affiant's statements were based on his "own personal knowledge and/or knowledge which he has been able to acquire upon inquiry." The affidavit was found inadequate because it failed to unequivocally show that that it was based on "personal knowledge" and because there was no representation that the facts disclosed were true.

So you should be careful in drafting an affidavit and not merely follow some form in a file, but think about what the document is supposed to do. Based on the Texas Supreme Court's reasoning, I offer this form for an affidavit:

<u>Affidavit of J. Trent Hamilton</u>

STATE OF TEXAS   §
                              §
COUNTY OF HARRIS   §

On this day J. Trent Hamilton personally appeared before me, and after I administered the oath, he stated:

> My name is J. Trent Hamilton and I am competent to make this affidavit. I have personal knowledge of the facts stated and they are true.
>
> [Body of affidavit contains the facts.]
>
> End of Affidavit.

_____
J. Trent Hamilton

Sworn to and signed before me by J. Trent Hamilton on [date].

_____
[seal]   Notary Public, State of Texas

Is there a reason to end an affidavit with "Further Affiant Saith Not"? I doubt it. It's probably not even necessary to state "End of Affidavit," but at least it's plainer language. Besides, you don't have to decide if it's spelled "saith" or "sayeth."

Certificate of Service

All rules of procedure will require a certificate by the attorney that a copy is being served on all parties, through their counsel of record. The problem is that some LAs simply state that a copy has been sent to all counsel on such-and-such a date. That's not acceptable.

Even though the rules may *not* so state, the better practice is to furnish complete information, including name and address at a minimum. If service is by fax, give the fax number. The *best* practice is to include all information on all parties—name, address, telephone and fax numbers, party represented, and method of service. Don't be complacent and think that the certificate of service must be prepared only once and then copied on all future pleadings. Lawyers move and change, and the certificate of service frequently needs updating.

I submit that the certificate of service should contain as much information as you have. Frequently, court clerks will use the certificate of service to contact parties to advise them of changes in a hearing, and they appreciate having all the information in one place.

Example of a proper certificate of service:

Certificate of Service

I certify that a copy of this motion has been served under Rules 21 and 21a, Texas Rules of Civil Procedure, on [date] on the following counsel of record:

Joe Blow, Attorney for [name of party]
[address, phone, fax]

Susan Donaldson, Attorney for [name of party]
[address, phone, fax]

[signature]

Keep a record of how you served it, whether by fax, personal delivery, or mail. This is especially critical if you are sending a notice. Don't let your lawyer get to the hearing and not have proof of service of the notice when a party doesn't show up. Also make sure you have checked your rules. A recent change to the Texas rules state that service by fax adds three days, just as service by mail. Sad, but true.

Cover Sheet

At this writing, a "Civil Cover Sheet" is required in federal court, and most state courts have some form that is required with the filing of any new suit. The cover sheet gives the clerks necessary information to enter into the computer. It is not a pleading. There is a box to be checked if the case is a jury or a nonjury case. This has been held by case law NOT to be a jury demand. The cover sheet is necessary, and you won't get your lawsuit filed without it, but don't make the mistake of thinking it is part of the actual pleading.

Summons

You will need to fill out an original and copy of a summons for each defendant, which will be signed by the clerk after your lawsuit is originally filed. Some state court clerks prepare the summons (called a "citation" in Texas) for you. In federal court you will also need a notice of lawsuit and request for waiver of service and a waiver of service of summons for the defendant to return. If not available from the clerk's office, they are in the federal appendix of forms.

Transmittal Letter

The transmittal letter is not a part of the pleading process, but in our daily lives, it is. Some courts file the transmittal letters; others don't. Some lawyers put substantive material in the transmittal letter; I sometimes wonder for whose benefit. If a court is to rule on a matter, it *must* be in the pleading. All rules will state somewhere that all dealings with the court will be through the clerk, and that direct communications with the court are not permitted. Therefore, the transmittal letter is generally for the benefit of the other parties.

If you are filing more than one document, list these—in a list, not strung out in a paragraph. This is as much for your own ease of checking to see what has been filed as for any other reason. When multiple items are strung out in a narrative paragraph, it is difficult to follow. Lists are a testament to your organizational skills.

The following is a skeleton form for a transmittal letter to a court clerk to file more than one document:

Example of Transmittal Letter

[Date]

[Name and address of clerk of court]

Re: [Number and name of case and court division)

Dear [name]:

Enclosed for filing on behalf of defendant Smith are:

1.   Response to Motion to Compel;
2.   Motion for Additional Discovery; and
3.   Notice of Hearing [date].

Please return a file-stamped copy by our waiting messenger.

[Closing and Signature]

cc: All parties as listed on certificate of service

Final Preparation for Filing

When the document is completed:

1.   Make sure the document is signed in all places;
2.   Check the local rules, which may require that two holes be
      punched at the top;
3.   Have the proper number of copies made for filing and file-
      stamping for return to your file; and
4.   Serve a copy on the other parties, as stated in your
      certificate of service.
5.   Include necessary cover sheets.
6.   Include prepared summonses or requests.
7.   Attach proper fee.
8.   Include extra copy for verification of filing.

In the next chapter, I discuss a few more details of these
documents you will be preparing and filing as the lawsuit progresses.

CHAPTER 7

General Remarks About Pleadings

Be Aware of the Trends

The trend is for states to amend their rules largely to conform with the federal rules. It might be one of the Naisbitts' "megatrends," that take many years to become the norm, but it is nevertheless a trend. The forms in this book will be for a civil case in federal court. In the not too distant future, all states (with the possible exception of Louisiana, which seems to thrive on doing *everything* differently) will have rules of procedure like the federal rules.

The Trend Toward Federal

The states follow changes made at the federal level. That's a historic fact and one reason the better practice is to learn the federal rules first. But for some reason, LAs learn state procedures well, but never bother to learn the federal rules. Then many are afraid of cases in federal court because they don't know anything about the rules!

Another reason to learn federal procedures first is that they're easy. They're simple. They make sense. They're well organized, as they appear in the order of a lawsuit's progression. The first rules are about filing and service, then responses and motions, then discovery, trial, post-trial, and appellate. What could be more logical? We are not so fortunate in our state rules, which seem to be thrown together and amended on whim.

Trend Toward Simplicity

The State Bar of Texas recently conducted a survey of state judges. Over 80 percent of them prefer a "radically simplified version of papers" filed in their court, according to Judge Lynn Hughes. I've shown you in earlier chapters what the federal government is doing to simplify the language in court opinions and statutes. Don't think that you will be criticized for brevity and clarity—unless it's by lawyers who insist on holding onto the past.

Trend Toward a Public Citation System

There is even a trend toward adopting public citation schemes rather than being forced to use West's copyrighted system. There are antitrust allegations and lawsuits about West's proprietary interest. Louisiana and Wisconsin are adopting such procedures and West's competitors certainly have no objection. West is pretty firmly entrenched, though, and to have different citation systems among our 50 states could be disastrous. Watch this movement closely, because it affects all of us. We already have competition between the Bluebook and the Maroon Book. To add even more disputes would make any effort toward uniformity impossible. But Ma Bell was broken up, the airlines were deregulated, and this, too, can happen. Hopefully, it will be worked out so that *simplicity* wins.

Changing Grammar Trends

In Chapter 5, I discussed the changing grammar trends, including sentences ending with prepositions, pronouns not agreeing with their antecedents, and elimination of some commas. One reason for change, in any field, is custom and usage. When rules are routinely ignored or violated, changes are made to accommodate usage. We must be aware of trends affecting our legal writing and our court procedures. The competent LA knows where to look, owns or has access to the necessary reference works, and remains aware of changes.

Practice Exercise: Engagement Letter

Before any litigation representation is undertaken, there should be an engagement letter between attorney and client. To practice editing and get a feel for making documents more concise, I've chosen an engagement letter actually used by a law firm. It's not the worst I've seen but it has many useless words and phrases, and it can be improved. Rather than throw it out and start over, I've used their format and tried to maintain the "flavor" of their letter. When revising another's work, it's a good idea to let it be recognizable as an edited version of their work. You don't want hard feelings.

First the firm's version (671 words) and then my edited version (444 words):

(1) Before editing (671 words)

[Date]

CONFIDENTIAL & PRIVILEGED

[ADDRESSEE]

Re: Engagement of [firm] in [name of litigation matter]

Dear _____:

We want to express our appreciation for engaging [firm] to represent you in _____ . The purpose of this letter is to set forth the terms of the engagement.

We will, of course, seek to conclude this matter as successfully and expeditiously as possible and will assign such personnel to the case as may reasonably be required in seeking to achieve this result. _____ and I will undertake most of the effort. However, we can make no representation, warranty or guarantee as to the outcome of any matter.

Our service billings are based on our current billing rates. My current rate is $xxx per hour and _____'s rate is $xxx per hour. Associates presently have rates ranging from $xx to $xxx per hour, and partner rates can range up to $xxx an hour (and in some instances with respect to very specialized services, $xxx). Paralegal assistance will be utilized as deemed necessary. Paralegals have billable rates from $xx to $xx per hour. These rates may be revised in the future.

We bill our clients on a monthly basis and, in addition to charges for services of paralegals and attorneys, our statements will include charges for long-distance telephone calls, photocopying, deliveries, telecopies, travel, filing fees and the like. In the event major ($500 or more for any one item) out-of-pocket expenses are incurred on behalf of a client, such as, for example, expert witness fees, court reporter fees, and the like, it is our firm's usual practice to forward such bills directly to our clients for payment. For expense items under $500, we normally pay such bills ourselves, and include those items in our next regular statement. Unless you prefer that a lower dollar amount be used as the dividing line, we will follow our usual practice as to expenses incurred on your behalf. In the event of an adverse judgment, you will also be responsible for the costs for any appeal bond or supersedeas bond (which may be in at least the amount of the judgment) that might be necessary to suspend enforcement of any adverse judgment before or during the appellate process. We are requesting that our statements be paid in full within 15 days after their receipt.

We will keep you advised of the status of the matters we are handling, and, of course, no settlement or compromise will be made without your approval and consent. You will be copied on all important correspondence and all pleadings before they are sent.

We have requested that you provide us with a $3,000.00 retainer. The retainer will be held as a deposit and applied to the final monthly bill. Any balance remaining at that time will be returned to you (although no interest will accrue to your benefit thereon). By execution of this engagement letter, you are acknowledging your understanding and acceptance of this engagement and are jointly and severally agreeing to make prompt payment of our statements with respect to this matter. Please make your retainer checks payable to [firm] and forward them to our accounting department.

Because the attorney-client relationship is a very personal one, we want you to understand that you have the right at any time, as do we, to terminate this engagement for any reason. In the event of termination before this matter is concluded, we shall make every reasonable effort to effect an orderly transfer of your files to whomever you may designate, provided however, that all of our fees and out-of-pocket expenses shall be fully paid.

Thank you again for engaging us to work for you. I hope this letter is of assistance to you in understanding our firm's fee arrangements and in setting forth our agreement. Please call if you have any questions or comments regarding it. I have enclosed two originals of this letter and I would appreciate it if you would sign both originals in the space provided below and return one to me in the enclosed envelope. In this way we will have a record of our agreed-upon fee arrangement.

Very truly yours,

_____

ACCEPTED AND AGREED:

_____
[Name]

(2) After editing (444 words)

[Date]

CONFIDENTIAL & PRIVILEGED

[ADDRESSEE]

Re: Engagement of [firm] in [name of litigation matter]

Dear _____:

We appreciate your engaging [firm] to represent [you or name of company] in this matter. This letter sets forth the terms of the engagement.

We will seek to conclude this matter as successfully and quickly as possible and will assign the necessary personnel to the case. Joe Blow and I will undertake most of the effort, and Andy Associate will assist. Of course, we make no representation or guarantee as to the outcome.

Invoices for services are based on our current billing rates. My current rate is $xxx per hour, Joe's is $xxx, and Andy's is $xxx. Other associates presently have rates ranging from $xx to $xxx. Paralegal assistance will be used as needed, and their billing rates are from $xx to $xx per hour. Any of these rates may be revised.

We will bill you monthly and, in addition to charges for services, our statements will include charges for long-distance telephone calls, faxes, photocopies, deliveries, travel, filing fees, and similar advanced costs. If there are major ($500 or more for any one item) out-of-pocket expenses, such as, for example, expert witness and court reporter fees, it is our firm's usual practice to send those bills directly to the client for payment. We will pay expense items under $500 and include those items in our next regular statement. Unless you prefer that a lower dollar amount be used as the dividing line, we will follow our usual practice. We request that our statements be paid in full within 15 days after receipt.

We will keep you informed of the status of the matters we are handling, and, of course, no settlement or compromise will be made without your approval and consent. We will send you copies of all important correspondence and pleadings.

Please send a $xxxx retainer payable to [firm]. The retainer will be held as a deposit and applied to the final monthly bill, with any balance being returned to you. By signing this engagement letter, you acknowledge your understanding and acceptance of this engagement and agree to make prompt payment of our statements.

The attorney-client relationship is a personal one. You have the right at any time, as do we, to terminate this engagement for any reason. If terminated before the matter is concluded, we will transfer your files to whomever you designate.

Thank you again for engaging us to work for you. I hope this letter helps you to understand our firm's fee arrangements and our agreement. Please call if you have any questions or comments. Please sign and return a copy of this letter to me, so that we will both have a record of our agreed-upon fee arrangement.

Very truly yours,

_____

ACCEPTED AND AGREED:

_____

[Name]

Do you disagree with any of the changes? Is the letter any less effective by being of 227 fewer words? Which one would sound better to you if you were the client? Which is easier to read? Is there any significant difference in meaning? Is it any less "legal" or binding?

Plaintiff's Pleadings: More Specifics

In pleading the plaintiff's cause of action, you must be specific enough to put the defendant on notice as to what he has allegedly done and what damage has been done because of it. The paragraphs should be consecutively numbered—arabic, not outline form with roman numerals. You may title the sections if helpful (Jurisdiction, Parties, Causes of Action, Negligence, Breach of Contract, Conspiracy, Antitrust, Damages, Prayer, etc.) but titles are not required.

After a brief opening paragraph, there are basically five areas to be covered.

Opening Paragraph. You opening paragraph can define how you will identify the parties throughout the pleading.

> *Plaintiff Jack Jones ("Jones") sues North Central Bank ("Bank") and states:*

I realize that's quite different from what you usually see. Opening paragraphs sometimes number well over a hundred words. (I doubt that it's even necessary to use the parenthetical defining. Won't the readers know who "Jones" is and who "Bank" is without being told?)

To make matters worse, many legal writers capitalize the *entire* names of the parties. That's not only unnecessary but very distracting. I have seen many pleadings with party *designations* (PLAINTIFF, DEFENDANT, INTERVENOR) in all caps all through the pleading. That is bad form because it disturbs the flow. The reader is accustomed to seeing all caps for *emphasis*, and it's distracting to have words in all caps appear throughout the document. However, if you insist on describing them by their party designation instead of their real-world capacity, it's hard to keep them separated, isn't it? (The reader may think, "Now, which one is plaintiff and which one is defendant and which one is third-party defendant, appellant, appellee," or whatever?) Why not just call them what or who they are so nobody gets confused?

And remember to use arabic-numbered paragraphs. No roman numerals. (Judge Hughes says, "Unless you can write your ZIP Code in roman numerals, right now, do not use them!")

(1) Jurisdiction. What is the source of the court's jurisdiction? Is it a federal question or is it diversity of citizenship? In state court, is it the amount in controversy or some other statute or rule? General reference to the federal statute is sufficient, but a better practice is to identify it by name or number. (You do not need to plead venue, because if venue is improper, it is up to defendant to raise it as an affirmative defense.)

This case involves diversity of citizenship, 28 United States Code, section 1334.

-or-

This case arises under [list the statute, article/section of the constitution, or the treaty].

The diversity statute contains the provision that diversity must be complete *and* that the amount in controversy must exceed $50,000. It is not necessary that you quote the *terms* of the statute. Just make sure your facts are correct.

More About Diversity

Diversity is an interesting feature of the federal rules. The LA needs to know about diversity. I want to give you some valuable tips that many lawyers don't even know. Prosecuting your suit in the best court is a critical factor when filing a lawsuit.

For federal jurisdiction under diversity of citizenship, diversity must be complete. *Complete diversity* means that the citizenship is completely different on both sides of the versus sign. For example:

Complete diversity:
  Texas citizen v. New Mexico citizen
  Illinois citizen v. Tennessee citizen
  Wisconsin citizen v. Texas citizen and a Louisiana citizen

Diversity not complete:
  Texas citizen v. New Mexico citizen and a Texas citizen
  Illinois citizen v. many defendants, one of whom is an Illinois citizen

What if the lawyer does *not* want the case in federal court? There will be times when you want to make sure that your case remains in state court. It may be because of more liberal juries, more favorable procedures, or any number of reasons. If you have filed a suit in state court and there is complete diversity of citizenship, as well as damages over $50,000, the defendant may remove the case to federal court. You may want to circumvent that possibility by making sure you have a local defendant so that diversity is not complete. I'm not talking about forum-shopping; I'm talking about considering all lawful and ethical options.

For example, if you are suing on an insurance contract, the carrier will probably be foreign, but the agent will probably be local. If you have grounds to sue the agent, then diversity will not be complete and the case cannot be removed. If the agent has been receiving notices, then the agent is "in the loop," and can be joined as a defendant.

A problem *can* arise even if diversity is not complete. For example, you have sued many defendants in a complex case. One of the defendants is local, making diversity incomplete. If the foreign defendants are *served* before the local defendant, that foreign defendant can remove the case to federal court because diversity is complete at that point. This is a tricky trap. You will want to make sure the local defendant has been served before the foreign defendants. This is one of those unfortunate procedural quirks that leads lawyers to manipulate the system. It needs to be changed. Check it carefully.

In state court you might simply state:

Damages exceed the jurisdictional limits of this court.
-or-
The amount in controversy exceeds the jurisdictional limits of this court.

(2) Statement of the case. This should be a short, concise description of what the lawsuit is about. One sentence should be enough.

This case involves violations of the antitrust statutes.

This case involves a real property boundary dispute.

This case involves a lawnmower that malfunctioned.

This case involves a car wreck.

This case involves a breach of contract.

(3) Identify the parties. If a party is a corporation or other entity other than an individual, describe it to answer the obvious questions, such as state of incorporation. You need only to give enough information for the party to be identified *to the exclusion of anyone else.* Since the rules require that service be *requested* to toll the statute of limitations, this is a good time to do it.

> *Smith is a citizen of Tennessee, residing in Shelby County. Acme is a Georgia corporation doing business in Tennessee. Acme can be served with process through its registered agent, CT Corporation System [address].*

(4) Describe the occurrence(s) or transaction(s) giving rise to the lawsuit. What happened in the real world? This is not the place for any sort of legal analysis, puffery, or expounding. Just give the reader notice of what happened. If a statute has been violated, state it.

Examples:

> *Robertson owes Madison $85,000 on the account attached as Exhibit A.*

> *Jones drove his car negligently and collided with the Smiths' car.*

Review the appendix of forms in the Federal Rules of Civil Procedure for guidance on how to state your case.

(5) Prayer. This does not have to be suitable for framing. Just list the particular relief, such as money, injunction, declaratory judgment, or whatever you seek. The forms in the federal appendix still use the word "wherefore" (but note, it's without a comma). It may be that we just cannot live without "wherefore" in our pleadings. But what would "wherefore" add to this prayer?

Jones claims:

1. *damages;*

2. *interest under the law;*

3. *punitive damages;*

4. *attorney's fees;*

5. *all other relief under the law.*

Defendant's Pleadings: Some Specifics

In state courts a "general denial" may be acceptable. If it is allowed, there probably is a rule of procedure addressing it, and you will need only to state it. That's sufficient.

Jones asserts a general denial under Rule 92, Texas Rules of Civil Procedure.

In federal court a general denial is not permitted. Each allegation in plaintiff's complaint is to be answered separately in the order given. Admit it, deny it, or explain it. Some attorneys like to say, "defendant is without sufficient information to either admit or deny paragraph 8 and therefore denies the same." No need for all those words. Just deny it, period.

2. *Acme admits paragraph 2.*

3. *Acme denies paragraph 3.*

For defendant's prayer, just ask that the claim be dismissed.

Bank prays that Smith's claims be dismissed.

Defendant might bring in a third-party defendant, saying, in effect, "maybe I did it, but if I did, XXX caused me to do it." For instance, in a three-car rear-end collision, plaintiff would be the front car, defendant and third-party plaintiff would be the middle car, and third-party defendant would be the back car. Substitute other kinds of tortfeasors and it's the same thing. The defendant becomes plaintiff in the third-party action. But we should still call them by their real-world names to avoid confusion. The third-party defendant might file a counterclaim against the defendant/third-party plaintiff, becoming a counterclaimant. I have seen pleadings which became so convoluted, nobody knew who anybody was. And some writers made a meticulous effort to call them by their correct—and *complete*—lawsuit capacities, even when it means a string of five or six of them! Why? There's no reason to deliberately confuse your reader.

Make sure you understand the difference between a counterclaim and a cross-claim. A counterclaim is between parties on opposite sides of the versus sign, and a cross-claim is between parties on the same side of the versus sign. Therefore, a defendant would have a *counterclaim* against the plaintiff but would have a *cross-claim* against another defendant.

Motions: More Specifics

If you plan to get someone's attention in a written communication, how do you do it? It's the same, no matter what it is—letter, thesis, speech. You must *involve* them from the beginning. Tell your audience what you want and then convince them that you should get it. With motions, we first state the *facts* that entitle us to the relief we are seeking, and then we state the *law* that backs up our position. You can do that in two short documents, a motion and a memorandum of authority, or you can combine them in one two-part document. If it's a long document, you definitely want to make it two separate documents. See Chapter 3 for Judge Hughes's excellent suggestions about motions.

Make the title useful and short. If it's agreed, include "Agreed" in the title.

Don't title it "Motion for Summary Judgment." Make it more specific:

Bank's Motion for Judgment on Limitations

Agreed Motion for Extension of Discovery

With motions, your main audience is the judge. In some cases, it's the law clerk who may be the first to read it. You must state, clearly and intelligibly, in the first paragraph what the problem is and what you want done about it.

First state **who** is doing the asking. "Acme Co." or better yet, "Acme"—not "Movant or "Plaintiff" or "defendant." Remember Judge Hughes's rules. Avoid such labels and use their real-world ID.

Next you want to **identify the bad guy** you want something from. You want Johnson to answer the interrogatories more fully. Or you want the bank to be prevented from getting records which are privileged.

Next, say **what** you want—*exactly*. Don't say you want the court to grant the motion. Say that you want the court to compel Johnson to produce his financial statements, or that you want the bank's pleadings stricken, or that you want costs assessed against the bad guy for the expenses of filing the motion, or some other *specific* sanction.

Furnish a "Notice of Motion." Check the rules for time limits. Check with the clerk for available dates. Some courts require that the notice be attached to the *front* of the motion. In the federal appendix of forms, the notice of motion appears after the motion and before the certificate of service. I doubt that you would be penalized for placement, but you *would* be penalized for failing to include a notice.

Make sure you state the **authority** on which your motion is based, which may be a particular rule of procedure. If you have colossally strong case precedent in a situation just like yours, add that as well. If the motion is complex, separate the motion from the authority: two pages for the motion and two pages for the memorandum in support. According to Judge Hughes, "If nothing else, they *look* shorter if they're separated."

Finally, attach an order stating what you want—exactly. The order should grant *specific* relief. Do not say "Plaintiff's motion is granted." Say, "Jones is given through [date] to respond to Acme's counterclaim." Make the order say exactly what you want the judge to rule. If the judge changes it, so be it. But many times the judge will sign it as presented.

Another reason to attach an order is so that the clerks will know to report the action. Many clerks' offices send cards or otherwise notify the parties that some action has been taken in a lawsuit. An order will trigger it. If the judge merely notes his ruling on his docket sheet, the clerk may not know about it.

A thoughtful detail would be to include telephone and fax numbers in your certificate of service. If the clerk needs to call all the parties, that is a big help. I think that it will be required in the rules in a very few years; why not just start it now?

Discovery

A big change came about several years ago when filing of discovery materials with the clerk was no longer permitted. The reason was simple: lack of storage space. This is a serious consideration and one which affects law firms as well. It is one of the reasons the courts changed from long paper to short paper: Letter-size file cabinets take up less room than the legal-size ones. Now the file cabinets are overflowing with motions and pleadings; they just will not hold volumes of discovery materials.

Now we have revolutionary changes that call for *mandatory* discovery. These sweeping changes in the federal discovery rules from January 1, 1994, will spill over to the states. They will help to curtail lawsuit abuse. Rule 26 now requires that discovery be exchanged *without a request*; this is called "Initial Disclosure."

Initial disclosure includes all those items that have been covered in our "boilerplate" requests for production of documents and interrogatories. It includes witnesses, documents, experts, and damage information, and must be exchanged by the parties by 14 days before the pretrial scheduling conference required by Rule 16. Read these new discovery rules! They are comprehensive and somewhat complicated. Don't be caught unaware: Know that the same changes to state rules will be close behind.

The new Rules 30 and 31 limit depositions (oral and written) to ten per party. The notice must state the method of taking as well as the name and address of the officer taking it. Times are shortened for depositions on written questions.

Interrogatories may not exceed 25, including subparts, under Rule 33. Grounds for objections must be specific.

Requests for admission under Rule 36 are serious, since failure to deny will conclusively establish a matter. When you receive or send requests for admission, calendar the 30 days in more than one place. I personally worked on an appeal to the Fifth Circuit because a case was *lost* when the lawyer failed to file responses within the 30 days. The opposing counsel had drafted excellent admissions, and the case was lost by the failure to deny them.

There are many new provisions in Rule 37 providing for sanctions to those parties failing to make disclosure or cooperate in discovery. Those sanctions include monetary fines assigned to both the parties and the attorneys as well as striking of pleadings. Sanctions are a serious matter, not to be taken lightly.

Judges are tired of being referees in discovery disputes. Lawyers who do not change their errant ways with respect to discovery will regret it. Before filing needless motions to compel, make a phone call, send a fax (or both). Before filing a request for extension of time, make an effort to communicate with opposing counsel. Lawyers should work out disputes instead of always running to the judge. Rambo-type lawyers counter judicial progress.

A Special Note About Summary Judgments

Motions for summary judgment are common. They are generally very complex, requiring abundant briefing, because summary judgment is a procedure based on the law, not facts. They will have many attachments, including affidavits (which may also have many attachments), discovery excerpts, admissions, and documents. Since a motion for summary judgment is complicated and well researched, as are responses, it is critical that the writing be clear and concise.

Summary: Just Think

In drafting pleadings, think about what you want and communicate it, clearly and concisely. Writing concisely does not mean short, choppy sentences. It does not mean boring, repetitive meter. It means thinking about what you are doing and eliminating unnecessary words and phrases. You can tell a story. You can offer quotations from masters. You can vary your sentence length. Remember to focus on the *reader*. Make it interesting. The forms in chapter 8 are for your guidance. Every case is different. Just think, organize clearly, and write concisely.

CHAPTER 8

Pleadings and Other Litigation Forms

An unmarried woman named Joyce Masterson comes to your office, without an appointment, and your attorney is out. She wants to file a lawsuit for a car wreck she had nearly two years ago. You call your attorney and he talks to her and asks her to give you the facts of the accident. He will call her when he returns to the office.

She relates the following: On June 2, 1993, she was driving alone in her 1990 Mercury Marquis Brougham and had stopped for a traffic light on South Durham Street at 20th in the Heights area of Houston, Harris County, Texas. While waiting for the light to change, she heard

109

tires screech, looked in her rear-view mirror, and saw a large red car careening out of control. It struck her from the rear.

She felt a hot flash of pain go down her spine and temporarily "saw stars." As she was coming to, she saw the red car back up, go around her, and flee the scene, but she got the license number. She pulled over, called 911, and a policeman arrived shortly. She gave him the details and he gave her the accident report number. A few days later, with the help of a deputy sheriff who was a friend, she learned the name and address of the driver. He had no insurance for his red 1979 Camaro.

Fortunately, her car was not totaled, but it cost $900 to have it repaired. She was not totaled, either, and had "only soft tissue injuries," but she did have to spend a week in the hospital and several months in physical therapy, losing her secretarial salary as well as overtime.

She has a $50,000 uninsured/underinsured provision in her auto policy, as well as $5,000 personal injury protection. Her insurance company has paid the $5,000 PIP, but no more. Suit must be filed against her insurance company, which will then "step in the shoes" of the uninsured driver of the red car.

If you can take these facts and prepare the first draft for your attorney's review, you will be very valuable to that attorney. Based on what you have learned so far of plain language principles, do you think you're ready to try? Remember: you need only put the defendant on notice as to the claim against it. Who will be the defendant in this case? Will you have to sue the defendant who didn't even have insurance? Probably not, but some states might require it. If the lawyer says to sue the insurance company, then that will be the only defendant. If the insurance company wants to bring in the driver, it can do so, can it not?

For now, we will assume that the client's insurance company will be the only defendant, and that the suit will be to recover under her uninsured motorist coverage, which she purchased for just such an event as this. Can you draft a plain language pleading in federal court based on these facts? I think you can, but in case you'd like a little help getting started, I have prepared one to get you going.

Here is a pleading you can draft for review by your attorney, and he just might file it with no changes:

IN THE UNITED STATES DISTRICT COURT
SOUTHERN DISTRICT OF TEXAS
HOUSTON DIVISION

JOYCE MASTERSON	§	
	§	
Plaintiff	§	CIVIL ACTION NO.
	§	
v.	§	_____
	§	
SELFISH INSURANCE CO.,	§	JURY
a corporation,	§	
	§	
Defendant	§	

COMPLAINT

Joyce Masterson sues Selfish Insurance Co. and states:

1.   Masterson is a citizen of Texas. Selfish is a Pennsylvania corporation that can be served through the Texas Commissioner of Insurance.

2.   This court has jurisdiction under Title 28, United States Code, section 1334.

2.   On June 2, 1993, while southbound in her car on Durham at 20th Street in Houston, Texas, Masterson was struck from the rear by an uninsured motorist.

3.   On that date, Masterson carried uninsured motorist coverage with Selfish.

4.   The collision caused Masterson personal injuries, property damage, and loss of earnings.

Masterson claims damages against Selfish for $50,000, plus her attorney's fees and lawful interest, and demands a jury for trial.

David Reynolds, 06800000
100 Main Street, Suite 100
Houston, Texas 77002-3737
(713) 555-9999 fax 555-9888
Attorney in Charge for
Joyce Masterson Plaintiff

OF COUNSEL:
Reynolds & Reynolds

That's all the complaint need say. You may get some argument from
your attorney, and it may go like this: "Oh, no, we have to put more in
it than that, because it's so hard to amend in federal court. You have to
get leave and maybe the judge won't grant it and we'd be up the creek."
See what I mean about a lawyer anticipating every little thing that can go
wrong? (Even when odds are they won't happen.)

In quoting from Bruce Catton, Judge Hughes once asked if anything
could make this allegation any more clear: "He farmed without
prospering." And the answer is no. Four words, crystal clear.

In this uninsured motorist case, everything will be produced in
discovery and proved at trial. This is a plain language pleading. You can
draft these pleadings for your attorney. If the attorney then adds a bunch
of legalese and unnecessary facts, so be it. You at least can draft
pleadings with an economy of words, and maybe, just maybe, the
practice will eventually sink in and become part of the attorney's way of
doing things. I have seen it work.

In drafting pleadings for your attorney, you will need to refer to
chapters 6 and 7, as well as the suggestions in this chapter. These forms
are for *guidance*. You will need to think. You should know your case
and draft pleadings based on the facts in your case. You do not have to
write in short, choppy sentences. You can vary your sentence length. But
always edit, and edit again to get rid of unnecessary formalisms,
repetition, and nonsense.

Most of these forms will be in federal court in Houston. I have
sprinkled in some forms from other federal jurisdictions as well as some
state court forms, so that you can note the similarities. I doubt that any
pleading would be refused by the clerk for any matter of form alone, so

even if you use these formats exactly, when your jurisdiction may have slightly different customs, the court clerk should accept it for filing. Again, I recommend that you take the time to visit your courthouse and check out some recent files and look at the format of those pleadings in your jurisdiction.

I have divided this final Chapter 8 into five sections, to help you find a needed form or get an idea:

A. Initial pleadings
B. Motions
C. Discovery
D. Appellate
E. Miscellaneous

I have not included every form you will ever need. No book could do that. These forms contain bare, plain language allegations. But after all that I have said, I do not advocate boring, "See Spot Run" writing. Your pleadings should not only be consise and clear, but colorful when possible. Changes are brought about by attention to extremes.

You can be ready when the call rings out:

"Prepare a motion to withdraw."

"Get me a motion for continuance."

"Respond to this motion for summary judgment."

"Draft an answer."

So I have included some of the forms you may be asked to prepare, as well as some obscure ones for variety. With some practice (and more practice, and editing), you can furnish everything else you may need as you stock your new plain language form files.

A. INITIAL PLEADINGS

Form: Shell of Original Pleading

IN THE UNITED STATES DISTRICT COURT
SOUTHERN DISTRICT OF TEXAS
HOUSTON DIVISION

JOHN SMITH	§	
	§	
Plaintiff	§	CIVIL ACTION NO.
	§	
v.	§	_____
	§	
EVIL TRUCKING CO.,	§	JURY
a corporation, and	§	
RICHARD BADD	§	
	§	
Defendants	§	

COMPLAINT

[Identity of parties, allegation of jurisdiction, causes of action, prayer.]

_____
James L. Scott (Identifying #)
Address
Phone, fax
Attorney in Charge for Plaintiff

OF COUNSEL:
(Firm name and
any other attorneys in the
firm working on the case)

JURY DEMAND

Plaintiff demands a jury.

Other Forms Needed to File a Lawsuit:

Accompanying plaintiff's complaint (in addition to the filing fee) will be the civil cover sheet, original and a copy of a summons for each party, notice of lawsuit and request for waiver of service of summons, and waiver of service of summons. You may obtain these forms from the clerk's office. If they are not available at your clerk's office, they also appear in the Appendix of Forms in the Federal Rules of Civil Procedure and you may copy them.

There is now a duty imposed by Rule 4 on a defendant in a lawsuit to avoid unnecessary costs of service of summons. If a defendant does not waive service, and does not show good cause for doing so, that defendant will be charged with the costs of service. This is another effort on the part of our government to lower the costs of and simplify litigation. It is not "good cause" for failing to waive service that the defendant believes the lawsuit to be bogus or the papers to be faulty. After the waiver is returned to you, file it with the clerk.

Form: Identifying the Parties

Jones is a citizen of Tennessee, residing in Shelby County. Acme is a Georgia corporation doing business in Tennessee. Acme can be served with process through its registered agent, [name and address].

Form: Allegation of Jurisdiction: Diversity of Citizenship

This case involves diversity of citizenship, 28 United States Code, section 1334.

Form: Allegation of Jurisdiction: Federal Question

This case arises under [list the statute, article/section of the constitution, or the treaty].

Form: Allegation of Jurisdiction: State Court

The amount in controversy in this case exceeds the jurisdictional limits of this court.

-or-

This case involves violation of the usury statutes [give statute numbers] [or other basis for state court jurisdiction].

Form: Verification

STATE OF TEXAS   §
                                   §
COUNTY OF HARRIS   §

On this day John Smith appeared before me, a notary public, and after I administered the oath, he stated that the facts in this motion are within his personal knowledge and are true.

_____
John Smith

Sworn to and signed by John Smith on [date].

[seal]   _____
                  Notary Public, State of Texas

Form: Corporate verification

STATE OF TENNESSEE   )
)
COUNTY OF HARDEMAN   )

     John Smith states on his oath that he is the [office held] of [name of corporation], that he has read the foregoing [title of document], that the matters stated are within his personal knowledge and are true, except those matters stated to be upon information and belief, and those he believes to be true, and that he is authorized by the corporation to sign this verification as the act of the corporation.

_____ [date]

_____ [signature]

Sworn to and signed before me by John Smith on [date].

[seal]   _____
                          [notary's signature and printed name]

Form: Affidavit

       Affidavit of [Name]

STATE OF TEXAS   §
                        §
COUNTY OF HARRIS   §

     On [date], [name] personally appeared before me, and after I administered the oath, he stated:

          My name is [name] and I am competent to make this affidavit. I have personal knowledge of the facts stated and they are true.

          [Body of affidavit contains the facts.]

          End of Affidavit.

_____
[Name]

Sworn to and signed before me by [name] on [date].

_____
[seal]   Notary Public, [jurisdiction]

Form: Acknowledgment

STATE OF TEXAS   §
                        §
COUNTY OF HARRIS   §

On this day John Smith appeared before me and acknowledged that he signed this [name of document].

_____
John Smith

Sworn to and signed by John Smith on [date].

_____
[seal]   Notary Public, State of Texas

Forms for Some Causes of Action

Form: Complaint for Negligence (car wreck)

#.   On [date] at the intersection of Park Avenue and Highland Street in Memphis, Tennessee, [plaintiff] was driving his car traveling north and [defendant] was driving his car traveling east.

#.   [Plaintiff] was legally in the intersection when [defendant] negligently entered the intersection against the light and struck [plaintiff].

#.   [Defendant's] negligence proximately caused the accident.

#.   As a result, [plaintiff] was injured and damaged as follows:

    a. her arm was broken and her face was cut;
    b. she suffered other injuries, some permanent;
    c. she lost earnings and the ability to earn;
    d. she suffered physical and mental pain;
    e. she incurred medical expenses of over $20,000; and
    f. she suffered property damage of $8,500.

Form: Complaint for Negligence (pedestrian/auto)

#.   On [date] in a public highway called Fannin Street in Houston, Texas, [defendant] negligently drove his car against [plaintiff], who was then crossing Fannin.

#.   As a result, [plaintiff] was thrown down and:

    a. his hip was broken;
    b. he suffered other injuries, some permanent;
    c. he was prevented from transacting his business;
    d. he suffered physical and mental pain;
    e. he incurred medical expenses of over $20,000; and
    f. he has past and future lost earnings.

Form: Complaint for Negligence under FELA

#.   During all relevant times defendant ICRR owned and operated in interstate commerce a railroad that passed through [location of accident].

#.   On [date of accident], ICRR was repairing the tracks at [location].

#.   In the course of the repairs on [date], ICRR employed plaintiff Smith as a workman, and negligently put Jones to work on a portion of the track left unprotected and unsafe by ICRR.

#.   Due to ICRR's negligence, Jones, while working as ordered by ICRR, was struck in the head by falling rock and suffered head and bodily injuries.

#.   Until these injuries, Jones was a strong, able-bodied man, earning $xxx per ____. By reason of these injuries he is incapable of gainful activity, has suffered mental and physical pain, and has incurred reasonable and necessary medical expenses of $xxxx.

Jones demands judgment against ICRR for $xxxx and costs.

Form: Complaint on an Account

#.   Jones owes Acme $xxxx according to the account attached as Exhibit A.

Form: Complaint for Goods Sold and Delivered

#.   [Defendant] owes [plaintiff] $xxxx for goods sold and delivered by [plaintiff] to [defendant] between [date] and [date].

Form: Request for Appointment of Receiver

#.   [Plaintiff] requests that a receiver be appointed to take possession of and administer [defendant's] assets, and that those assets be reduced to money and distributed among [plaintiff] and other creditors entitled to payment.

Form: Complaint for Breach of Contract

#.   On [date] Smith and Jones signed a contract with Jones agreeing to pay Smith $5,000 for work performed by Smith. A copy of the contract is attached as Exhibit A.

#.   Smith performed the work called for in the contract but Jones has failed to pay, despite demands by Smith.

#.   As a result of Jones's failure, Smith was damaged for the loss of the $5,000, the loss of earnings on the $5,000, and the loss of other contracts.

Form: Complaint on a Promissory Note

#.   On [date] Jones signed and delivered to Smith a promissory note, promising to pay $xxxx by [date]. A copy of the note is attached as Exhibit A.

#.   Jones has failed, despite demands, to pay the note and owes Smith the amount of the note plus interest.

Form: Complaint for Patent Infringement

#. On [date] United States Letters Patent No. xxx were issued to [plaintiff] for a [invention], and [plaintiff] still owns the patent.

#. [Defendant] has infringed those letters patent by manufacturing and selling products using the patented invention, and will continue doing so unless enjoined by this court.

#. All proper notices have been posted and given.

#. [Plaintiff] has been damaged by [defendant's] infringement.

[Plaintiff] demands a preliminary and final injunction against continued infringement, an accounting for damages, and all damages, with interest and costs, against [defendant].

Form: Application for Temporary Restraining Order

#. [Plaintiff] seeks an order preventing [defendant] from disbursing funds held in the name of xxx.

#. It is likely that [plaintiff] will recover from defendant because [state reason].

#. If this application is not granted, harm to [plaintiff] is imminent and is irreparable because [state the reasons].

#. [Plaintiff] has no adequate remedy at law because [defendant] is insolvent [other appropriate reason].

#. There is insufficient time to serve notice on [defendant] and hold a hearing on this application.

Note: a bond will be needed for restraining order or injunction.

Form: Request for Temporary Injunction

#.   [Plaintiff] requests a hearing on its application for temporary restraining order and that, after hearing, the court issue a temporary injunction against [defendant].

Form: Temporary Restraining Order

1.   On [date], the court heard [plaintiff's] application for temporary restraining order and finds, after examining the pleading and affidavits, that there is evidence that:

  a.   [Plaintiff] will recover from [defendant];

  b.   Harm is imminent and without the temporary restraining order, [plaintiff] will be irreparably injured because [state reason]; and

  c.   This ex parte order is necessary without notice to [defendant] because of insufficient time to notify [defendant] and hold a hearing.

2.   It is ordered:

  a.   [Defendant] is restrained from [as requested];

  b.   The clerk will issue notice to [defendant] that the hearing on [plaintiff's] application for temporary injunction is set for [date] at [time]. The hearing will be to determine if this temporary restraining order should be made a temporary injunction pending trial on the merits; and

  c.   [Plaintiff] will post a bond of $xxxx.

This order expires on [date].

Signed on [date] at [time].

[Signature of judge]

Note: as a practical matter, the judge may ask defendant's attorney to come over for a hearing.

Form: Complaint for Declaratory Judgment

#.   This is a dispute over coverage under an insurance policy issued by [defendant] to [plaintiff]. [State the policy terms sued upon.]

#.   [Name or occurrence] is therefore covered under the policy, and [plaintiff] requests judgment:

      a. Declaring [state the relief sought];

      b. Awarding [plaintiff's] reasonable attorney's fees;

      c. Awarding [plaintiff's] reasonable costs.

Form: Shell of Plaintiff's Subsequent Pleadings

IN THE UNITED STATES DISTRICT COURT
SOUTHERN DISTRICT OF TEXAS
HOUSTON DIVISION

JOHN SMITH	§	
	§	CIVIL ACTION NO.
	§	95-6739-CV
	§	
v.	§	
	§	
EVIL TRUCKING CO.,	§	
et al.	§	JURY

<u>(TITLE OF PLEADING)</u>

(Body of pleading)

[Signature block]

CERTIFICATE OF SERVICE

I certify that a copy has been served on [date] on the following counsel of record:

Mr. Steve Stevens, by fax to (214) 555-7777
(address and telephone)
Attorney for _____

Mr. John Johnson, by mail
(address, fax and phone)
Attorney for _____

_____
Attorney in Charge for Plaintiff

Form: Motion for Substituted Service

Check your state court procedures. Unlike federal procedures, state courts frequently require service by the sheriff or some other public official, and private service is authorized only in certain instances.

1.   [Plaintiff] requests substitute service on [defendant] because service by [method] has been unsuccessful.

2.   Defendant can be served at [list all addresses you have].

3.   [Plaintiff] requests authorization to serve [defendant] by leaving a copy of the citation and petition with [state per statute or state other alternative method].

4.   Affidavit of [name] is attached as Exhibit A.

Form: Order for Substituted Service

On [date] the court considered [plaintiff's] motion for substituted service and supporting affidavit and finds that the requested substituted service will be effective to give [defendant] notice of this suit.

It is ordered that [plaintiff's] motion is granted and that substituted service on [defendant] is authorized by [state the method of service].

Signed [date].

[Signature of judge]

Form: Order Authorizing Service Under Rule xxx

The court may have a rule authorizing an approved list of private process servers. If so, you may need only this order and no motion.

The court finds that [name] is of lawful age, not a party to this suit, is not interested in the outcome of the suit, and is authorized to serve process on [defendant].

Signed [date].

[Signature of judge]

Form: Shell of Answer

UNITED STATES DISTRICT COURT
EASTERN DISTRICT OF WISCONSIN

JOHN DOE

Case No. 95-6739-CV

v.

MARY SMITH

ANSWER OF MARY SMITH

(Body of pleading)

Dated at _____, Wisconsin, [date].

Law Firm Name
Attorneys for [Party]

By:_____
(Attorney's name and State Bar number)

Law firm address
and phone number

CERTIFICATE OF SERVICE

I certify that a copy has been served on [date] on the following counsel of record:

Mr. Joe R. Blow (address)
Attorney for Plaintiff

_____
[Attorney signing]

Form: Defendant's Answer and Defenses

    #.   [Defendant] admits paragraph 1.

    #.   [Defendant] denies paragraphs 2 through 5.

First Defense: Statute of Limitations

    #.   The acts complained of did not accrue within two years of filing the suit.

Second Defense: Contributory Negligence

    #.   [Plaintiff's] conduct contributed to her injuries.

Form: Defendant's Rule 12b Motion

Note: Motions under Rule 12 are filed BEFORE the answer. For purposes of statutory time to file a jury demand, Rule 12 motions are not "pleadings to the triable issue."

[Defendant] moves the court:

1.   To dismiss the action because the complaint failed to state a claim against [defendant] upon which relief can be granted;

2.   To dismiss the action because [defendant] has not been properly served with process, as evidenced by the affidavit of [name] attached as Exhibit A; and

3.   To dismiss the action because the court lacks jurisdiction because the amount in controversy is less than $50,000.

Form: Motion to Transfer Venue

#. This court is not the proper venue for this suit because:

the accident occurred in [place]

-or-

the contract was signed in [place]

-or-

[state the reason]

#. Venue of this suit is proper in [state the jurisdiction, district, or county].

#. [Defendant] requests that this case be transferred to [place].

Form: Counterclaim

#. [Plaintiff] is indebted to [defendant] for $xxxx because of [state the reason or grounds].

-or-

#. The accident was caused by [plaintiff's] negligence and [defendant] claims property damage of $xxxx.

-or-

#. [Plaintiff] is liable to [defendant] because he breached his fiduciary duty to [defendant].

-or other appropriate basis-

Form: Cross-Claim [*between parties on same side of versus sign*]

    #.   The accident was caused by [codefendant's] negligence and [this defendant] claims property damage of $xxxx.

Form: Affirmative Defenses

    #.   [Defendant] is not liable to [plaintiff] because:

    [Select appropriate defenses, which might include]:

    accord and satisfaction
    arbitration and award
    assumption of risk
    collateral estoppel
    contributory negligence
    discharge in bankruptcy
    duress
    estoppel
    failure of consideration
    failure to mitigate damages
    fraud
    illegality
    immunity
    laches
    mutual mistake
    payment
    preexisting condition
    privilege
    promissory estoppel
    release
    res judicata
    statute of frauds
    statute of limitations
    usury

B. Motions

Tip: Always prepare and send the court an order granting the relief you request in the motion.

Form: Shell of Motion

UNITED STATES DISTRICT COURT
FOR THE MIDDLE DISTRICT OF FLORIDA
TAMPA DIVISION

JOHN SMITH   :   CIVIL ACTION NO.
                            :   95-8432-CV

v.   :

EVIL TRUCKING CO.,   :
et al.   :

(TITLE OF MOTION)

(If it is an "Unopposed" motion, call it "Unopposed Motion for etc." Check local rules if the word "Unopposed" must appear in the caption.)

(If "Opposed," call it "Opposed Motion for [whatever]" Also check local rules for submission day. Prepare notice. If the attorney needs oral argument and it is permitted under the local rules, schedule it with the court coordinator, and include it in the notice.)

(Body of motion, **INCLUDING AUTHORITY**)

Also, if the motion is opposed, and if it is a motion other than for summary judgment, check the local rules. They might require the following language:

This motion is opposed. Movant has conferred with (name opposing counsel) and (has been advised that the motion is opposed) or (counsel cannot agree about the disposition of this motion).

[Signature block, stating name of firm,
Address, telephone, and party represented

By: {name}
Trial Counsel]

Tip: A notice should accompany a motion. It may be a notice of submission or a notice of hearing, depending on procedures of the particular court. Always check the local rules, which may require that the notice be attached in front of the motion.

NOTICE OF SUBMISSION

TO: ALL COUNSEL OF RECORD AS LISTED IN CERTIFICATE OF SERVICE BELOW:
[or name them here]

Please take notice that this motion will be submitted to Judge [Name] on [date], without notice from the clerk and without appearance by counsel.

-or-

This is notice that the attached motion will be considered by the court on [date] without oral argument.

-or-

This is notice that the attached motion will be heard in the [name of court] Court at [address] on [date] at [time].

CERTIFICATE OF SERVICE

I certify that copies of this motion and notice have been served on [date] on the following counsel of record:

Mr. Steve Stevens, by fax to (214) 555-7777
(address)
Attorney for _____

Mr. John Johnson, by hand delivery
(address)
Attorney for _____

_____
(Name of Attorney in Charge)

Form: Shell of Proposed Order Granting Motion

IN THE UNITED STATES DISTRICT COURT
SOUTHERN DISTRICT OF TEXAS
HOUSTON DIVISION

JOHN SMITH	§	CIVIL ACTION NO.
	§	
	§	_____
v.	§	
	§	
EVIL TRUCKING CO.,	§	JURY
et al.	§	

ORDER

Smith's motion for _____ is granted and [state the particular relief granted as specifically as possible].

SIGNED: [Date]

_____
UNITED STATES DISTRICT JUDGE

Form: Shell of Response to Motion

IN THE UNITED STATES DISTRICT COURT
FOR THE NORTHERN DISTRICT OF ILLINOIS
EASTERN DIVISION

JOHN SMITH   )
)
) No. 95 C 9999
v.   )
) [Name of Assigned Judge]
EVIL TRUCKING CO.,   )
et al.   )

RESPONSE TO MOTION FOR _____

(Body of response, **INCLUDING AUTHORITY**)

EVIL TRUCKING CO.

By: _____
                One of Its Attorneys

_____
[Name of individual attorney]
ARDC # _____
Firm name
Firm address
Firm phone and fax numbers

[Certificate of Service]

Form: Shell of Proposed Order Denying Motion

IN THE UNITED STATES DISTRICT COURT
SOUTHERN DISTRICT OF TEXAS
HOUSTON DIVISION

JOHN SMITH	§		CIVIL ACTION NO.
	§		
	§		_____
v.	§		
	§		
EVIL TRUCKING CO.,	§		JURY
et al.	§		

ORDER

Smith's motion for _____ is denied.

SIGNED: _____, 19__.

_____
UNITED STATES DISTRICT JUDGE

Form: Shell of Rule 50 Motion in Federal Court

(formerly called a Motion for Directed Verdict or a Motion for Judgment Notwithstanding the Verdict or Motion for Judgment Non Obstante Veredicto) ***(***Do not use the outdated language***)***

IN THE UNITED STATES DISTRICT COURT
SOUTHERN DISTRICT OF TEXAS
HOUSTON DIVISION

JOHN SMITH	§	CIVIL ACTION NO.
	§	
	§	_____
v.	§	
	§	JURY
EVIL TRUCKING CO.,	§	
et al.	§	

MOTION FOR JUDGMENT AS A MATTER OF LAW

(In a jury trial, we no longer have to wait until the close of the evidence to move for judgment. It can be done at any time before the case is submitted to the jury. May be granted by the court after a party has been fully heard on an issue when there is no legally sufficient evidence for a reasonable jury to find for that party. Must be specific regarding the law and facts on why the party is entitled to judgment.)

(Body of motion, **INCLUDING AUTHORITY**)

[Signature block]

[Certificate of Service]

Form: Third-Party Complaint

#.   [Plaintiff] has filed against [defendant] a complaint, copied as Exhibit A.

#.   [Grounds on which defendant is entitled to recover from third-party defendant, formatted as a complaint.]

[Defendant] demands judgment against [third-party defendant] for all sums that may be adjudged against [defendant] in favor of [plaintiff].

Form: Motion to Bring in Third-Party Defendant

[Defendant] moves for leave, as third-party plaintiff, to serve on [third-party defendant] a summons and third-party complaint, copies of which are attached as Exhibit A.

Form: Motion to Quash Service of Process

[Defendant] requests that the court quash service of process on him because:

a. There are jurisdictional defects in the complaint;

b. The summons is defective because [reason];

c. It was not served by a disinterested person; or

d. [Other appropriate reason].

Form: Motion to Abate

[Defendant] requests that the court abate the proceedings pending in this county because [plaintiff] sued first in [name of other county] and that court has dominant jurisdiction.

-or-

[Defendant] requests that the court abate these proceedings because the parties have agreed to arbitrate this dispute.

-or-

[appropriate grounds]

Motions for Summary Judgment

Special note about summary judgment proceedings:

A summary judgment may be rendered on any claim when there is no genuine issue of material *fact* and the moving party should prevail as a matter of *law* (if a trial were held on the matter). It does not always dispose of the entire case, but perhaps only a part of the case. (It can dispose of the *entire* case, however.) If there is a fact issue, summary judgment will not be granted. In defending a summary judgment, you want to try to point out or raise a fact issue.

The purpose of the procedure is to save time for courts and litigants, to delineate matters to be resolved at trial, and to assess the proof to determine if there is really a need for trial.

Of critical importance to the LA is to calendar accurately the timetable for summary judgment procedures. There are strict rules governing amount of notice to be given and dealines for filing responses.

Form: Motion for Summary Judgment on Liability

  #.   [Plaintiff] requests a summary judgment as to [defendant's] liability because each element of her cause of action has been proved or stipulated.

  #.   Attached as evidence are [affidavits, deposition excerpts, interrogatory answers, etc.)

  #.   [Authority]

  #.   There are no fact issues.

Form: Defendant's Motion for Summary Judgment

  #.   [Defendant] is entitled to summary judgment on its counterclaim because he can prove every element of his counterclaim as a matter of law. [Authority.]

  #.   Attached is [defendant's] summary judgment proof:

       [Here list the proof, whether affidavits, deposition testimony, interrogatory answers, stipulations, etc.]

Form: Motion for Summary Judgment on Coverage

  AAA Insurance Company ("AAA"), under Federal Rule of Civil Procedure 56, moves for partial summary judgment on coverage and states:

Summary of Motion

This suit involves a dispute over coverage under an insurance policy (see amended complaint attached as Exhibit A). Plaintiff XYZ Corp. ("XYZ") and defendant Widget Corp. ("Widget") were defendants in a suit by Jolly Roger in the 280th District Court of Harris County, Texas ("the Roger suit"). AAA defended Widget under an insurance policy. Limited insurance was extended to XYZ under a vendor's endorsement to that policy, and XYZ declined. XYZ also failed to comply with the policy's provisions and cannot require AAA now to provide that coverage. AAA is entitled to summary judgment on the issue of coverage as a matter of law.

(Background)

(Standard for Summary Judgment, with authority)

(Policy Requirements Not Satisfied, with authority)

(Insured's Duties, with authority)

(Vendor's Endorsement Excludes Coverage, with authority)

Conclusion

For these reasons, AAA's motion should be granted and the court should declare that, as a matter of law, AAA had no duty to defend XYZ under the insurance contract and that AAA did not breach the contract.

[Signature Block]

[Certificate of Service]

[Summary judgment proceedings are generally excluded from requirement for certificate of conference.]

[Notice of Hearing/Submission]

Form: Response to Motion for Summary Judgment

    #.   The court must view the summary judgment evidence in a light most favorable to the nonmovant, indulging every reasonable inference in favor of nonmovant. [Authority.]

    #.   There is a genuine issue of material fact [describe it].

    #.   The court should deny [party's] motion for summary judgment because [party] failed to establish it was entitled to a summary judgment as a matter of law.

Form: Motion for Rehearing

There are some rare times when a motion for rehearing is worthwhile. One would be when a new decision has come down that may change the court's ruling.

[Party] asks the court for a rehearing on the order granting summary judgment on the issue of [state the basis] because:

    #.   After oral argument the Supreme Court issued its opinion in *Johnson v. Barber*, [citation and date]. A copy is attached.

    #.   The facts of this case are nearly identical to the *Johnson* case and a rehearing would serve justice in light of this decision.

[Party] requests that the court withdraw its order granting summary judgment and set a hearing for additional argument.

Form: Motion for Nonsuit

#.   [Party] asks the court to enter a nonsuit on all its claims against [party].

#.   [Party's] nonsuit will not prejudice the rights of remaining parties.

Form: Notice of Nonsuit

#.   [Party] files a nonsuit on all its claims against [party].

#.   [Party's] nonsuit will not prejudice the rights of remaining parties.

Form: Stipulation of Evidence

Plaintiff and defendant have agreed:

(List the things stipulated.]

Form: Order on Stipulation of Evidence

On [date] plaintiff and defendant presented the attached stipulations to the court. After review, the court finds that the stipulations should be received into evidence.

The court admits the attached stipulations into evidence and orders that no party need offer proof of the facts in the stipulations.

Signed [date].

[Signature of Judge]

Form: Motion in Limine

[Party] urges this motion in limine to avoid prejudice and a possible mistrial. If [adverse party] injects the following matters into the trial of this cause, whether through a party, attorney, or witness, [party] will suffer irreparable harm that cannot be cured by a jury instruction.

The matters will be adapted to the particular facts and type of lawsuit, but may include the following:

1. Any evidence not produced in discovery

2. Testimony of experts' discussions with other experts

3. Matters regarding religion

4. Evidence of [party's] [prior behavior, drinking habits, or other irrelevant conduct]

5. Evidence of criminal convictions

6. Privileged matters

Form: Motion for Continuance

[Party] asks the court to continue the trial of this case until after [date]. [State the grounds, which may include:

{Party} needs additional depositions {list them}.

{Witness} has been unavailable for deposition and his testimony is necessary. {Party} expects {witness} to testify to the following: {state the salient points and what will be proved}.

A death in the immediate family of {party or counsel} makes it impossible for him to attend the trial on {date}.

This request is not for delay but that justice may be done.
[The rules may require that you attach a verification.]

Form: Motion for ADR

Alternative Dispute Resolution is so successful these days that you may never need this form, because judges, on their own, are assigning cases to mediation with increasing frequency. This is good for the legal system. If that doesn't happen, here is a form.

[Party] asks the court to assign this case to mediation, nonbinding arbitration, or other alternative dispute resolution procedure.

[If the parties have agreed on a mediator, state the name and address and ask that the court approve.]

Form: Agreement to Mediate

The parties have agreed to mediate this case and Andrew C. Lawyer has been designated as the mediator.

It is agreed:

1.   Andrew C. Lawyer is authorized to conduct the mediation in this case.

2.   The mediation will be governed by [statutory provision] and this agreement.

3.   The mediation sessions will be private, confidential, and privileged from discovery.

Form: [Party's] Formal Bill of Exceptions

On [date], during trial the court ruled [describe the action excepted from].

[Party] excepted in open court to the ruling.

[Party] files this bill of exception to be included in the case record.

[Date]
                    [Signature of attorney]

Form: Final Judgment [nonjury trial]

On [date] this case was called for trial and the parties appeared and announced ready. The court determined that it had jurisdiction over the parties and the subject matter, that a jury had been waived, and the case proceeded to trial. All factual and legal matters were submitted and the court heard evidence and arguments of counsel. The court finds for [party] and orders:

1.   [Party] recover from [party] $[amount], interest at [#] per cent annually, and all costs.

2.   [Party] asked for and proved attorney's fees of $[amount], and the court orders [party] to pay [party] $[amount] for attorney's fees through the trial, $[amount] if appealed to the court of appeals, and $[amount] if appealed to the supreme court of [state].

All relief not granted in this final judgment is denied.

Signed [date].
                    [Signature of judge]

Form: [Party's] Request for Findings of Fact and Conclusions of Law

The court signed a judgment on [date].

This request is filed within the proper statutory time limit.

[Party] asks the court to enter findings of fact and conclusions of law.

[Sometimes you may need to prepare them and attach your suggested Findings of Fact and Conclusions of Law to the request.]

Form: Final Judgment [jury trial]

On [date] this case was called for trial and the parties appeared and announced ready. The court determined that it had jurisdiction over the parties and the subject matter, and impaneled and swore the jury. The case proceeded to trial and the jury heard the evidence and arguments of counsel. The court submitted questions and instructions to the jury and the jury made its findings on those questions. The jury's findings were filed in this record and incorporated in this final judgment by reference.

It is therefore ordered:

1.   [Party] recover from [party] $[amount], interest at [#] per cent annually, and all costs.
                              -or-
1.   [Plaintiff] take nothing by this suit and that [defendant] recover from [plaintiff] his costs for defending this suit.

[List other necessary provisions per the verdict and applicable statutes.]

All relief not granted in this final judgment is denied.

Signed [date].
                    [Signature of judge]

Form: Application for Turnover Order

Does your state have a turnover statute? It may.
Texas does, and there is also a federal one.
Here is a form to guide you.

APPLICATION FOR TURNOVER ORDER

Plaintiff XYZ applies for an order to collect the judgment against Herman Smith, judgment debtor, in this case under section 31.002 of the Texas Civil Practice & Remedies Code.

1.   XYZ was awarded a judgment against Smith on [date] for $xxxxx, plus attorney's fees of $xxx, interest at 10 percent, and all costs of court.

2.   Smith may be served with the turnover order at [address].

3.   The judgment is final and unsatisfied. A copy is attached as Exhibit A.

4.   Smith possesses property not exempt from execution for the satisfaction of liabilities, that cannot be readily attached by legal process: [describe the property, such as a bank account, accounts receivable, interest in a judgment in the case of [name, number, court, and date], copy of which is attached as Exhibit B] ("the property").

5.   XYZ is entitled to assignment of Smith's interest in that property to satisfy Smith's debt to XYZ in this case.

6.   XYZ has incurred attorney's fees in filing this application and under section 31.002(d) is entitled to recover $2,500.

Prayer

XYZ requests an order granting this application and ordering the following:

1.   That the clerk issue a writ of execution commanding the Harris County sheriff or constable to seize the property

from Smith and to forward all relevant documents and records to the court registry pending delivery to XYZ;

2.   That the property be stored for ten days so that all parties may examine the property under court supervision;

3.   That all costs of this turnover proceeding, including attorney's fees, be awarded to XYZ;

4.   That on final consideration of this application, the court order the property transferred to XYZ.

[Signature block, etc. and appropriate order]

Form: Motion for New Trial

[Party] requests a new trial as required by [identify the statute] because:

[State the grounds, which may include the following:

The court erred in granting summary judgment because {party} did not meet its burden {etc.};

The court abused its discretion in not allowing {party} to amend its pleadings;

The court abused its discretion by denying {party's} motion for a continuance;

[Party] discovered material, admissible, competent evidence after trial that could not have been discovered sooner because [reason] and that probably would have produced a different trial result;

The court abused its discretion in excluding {testimony, evidence, etc.}.]

C. Discovery

Caveat: Discovery matters should be worked out between the lawyers whenever possible. With the liberal discovery rules and mandatory disclosure provisions, discovery paper should decrease significantly. You will certainly send interrogatories, requests for admission and production, and deposition notices. But even those matters should be worked out and voluntarily produced. Motions to compel discovery should be rare. Motions for video or telephone depositions should not have to be used. Those matters should be worked out without judicial intervention. That's not always possible, though, and here are some forms for your use and adaptation.

Tip: Court reporters generally have forms for deposition notices. They also have forms for depositions on written questions, which are frequently used for custodians of records. You will need only to send the particular questions to be asked. Just remember that depositions on written questions take longer to complete than an oral deposition (generally 30 days to answer and additional time for ross-questions).

Form: Business Record Affidavit

STATE OF TEXAS   §
COUNTY OF HARRIS   §

Before me personally appeared [name], who after being sworn by me, stated:

My name is [name]. I am competent to make this affidavit and have personal knowledge of these facts.

I am the custodian of records of [name of business]. Attached are xx pages of records from [business]. These records are kept by [business] in the regular course of business. It was the regular course of business that an employee or agent of [business] recorded or transmitted information to be included in the record, and the record was made at the same time or shortly after. The attached records are originals or exact duplicates.

[Signature of affiant]

Sworn to and signed before me by [name] on [date].

[Signature/seal of notary public]

Form: Notice of Deposition

Note: if the deponent is a party, it is sufficient to serve the notice on his attorney. If not a party, the notice is served on all counsel of record and the deponent must be served with a subpoena. The notice is served first.

To: [Adverse party], through his attorney [name]
       [Attorney's address]

Please take notice that [party] will take the oral deposition of [deponent and address] on [date] at [time] before [reporter's name and address]. [If video, add:] The deposition will also be video taped by [videographer's name and address]. The deposition will continue from day to day until completed.

[Requesting party] requests that deponent produce the following documents at the deposition: [list them as specifically as possible].

Form: Motion for Leave to Take Additional Depositions

[Party] asks permission to take three depositions more than the ten permitted by Rules 26, 30, and 31, Federal Rules of Civil Procedure.

The ten depositions already taken in this case have raised new issues: [state them].

[Party] seeks to depose [names and addresses], who will testify concerning [subject matter], and opposing counsel refuses to agree.

Form: Stipulation for Additional Discovery

The parties agree:

\#.   That ten depositions have already been taken in this case;
\#.   That [#] additional depositions are needed, of [names and addresses of deponents];
\#.   That these additional depositions may be taken by telephone.

Form: Motion for Telephone Deposition

[Party] asks the court to permit him to take the telephone deposition of [deponent], as permitted by Rule 30(b)(7) of the Federal Rules of Civil Procedure *[or, if in state court, the state court rule: Rule 202 of the Texas Rules of Civil Procedure]*.

\#.   [Deponent] is located at [residence or work city/address].

\#.   A telephone deposition would save expenses of all parties in traveling to [deponent's city] and will be more convenient for [deponent].

Form: Request for Commission to Take Deposition of [Name] in [Foreign Jurisdiction]

[Party] asks the court to issue a commission to [name/address of officer] to take the deposition of [deponent's name and address], as allowed by [rule of procedure].

#.   [Deponent] is outside the jurisdiction of this court and his deposition is necessary to the trial of this case.

#.   [Officer] is permitted to take a deposition under [statute or rule]. The deposition will be taken with all necessary formalities and requirements.

Form: Commission to Take Deposition of [Deponent] in [Place]

To: [Name and address of officer taking deposition]

You have been commissioned by the court and are authorized to take the oral deposition of [deponent] residing at [address]. The deposition is for evidence solely for use at trial of this case.

By this commission you are ordered to:

1.   Issue a subpoena for deponent to appear as a witness in this case, at a time and place designated by the parties;

2.   Administer the oath to deponent;

3.   Transcribe the proceedings and reduce them to writing;

4.   Mark exhibits; and

5.   Certify the accuracy of the transcript, seal it, the exhibits, and a copy of this commission, and send it to the party asking the first question and to all parties requesting copies.

This commission is authorized by court order signed on [date].

Signed [date].

[Signature of Clerk of the Court]

Form: Interrogatories

(Limited to 25, including "all discrete subparts")

To: [Party] through [attorney/address]

Under Rule 33, Federal Rules of Civil Procedure, answer the following questions:

1. [Question]

Answer:

2. [Question]

Answer:

[Continuing through certificate of service]

Form: Requests for Admission

[Note: Requests for Admission, NOT Request for Admissions]

To: [Party] through [attorney/address]

Under Rule 36, Federal Rules of Civil Procedure, admit or deny the following:

Request 1: [That Joe Blow was driving the yellow car in the collision in this suit.]

Response:

[Continuing with what you want to be admitted. Responses are not under oath.]

If there is no response within the statutorily prescribed time, the admissions are deemed admitted. A motion to deem is not required; they are simply deemed admitted. For this reason, requests for admission are critical. As soon as your office receives them, every calendar should be noted so that they are responded to within the proper time—probably 30 days. If they are deemed admitted against your firm's client, you might want to move to strike the deemed admissions. Good luck, because it's difficult to do. But here's a form to guide you.

Form: Motion to Strike Deemed Admissions

[Party 1] asks the court to strike deemed admissions, as permitted under [rule of procedure].

1.   [Party 2] served her requests for admission on [date]. [Party 1] failed to file responses and the requests were deemed admitted. Good cause exists to strike the deemed admissions, and [party 1] asks that the court strike the admissions and allow him to file the attached responses.

2.   A court may strike deemed admissions, for good cause. [Authority.]

3.   [State the reason for not responding.]

4.   [Party 2] will not be prejudiced if the court strikes the admissions.

For these reasons and by the quoted authority, [party 1] asks the court to grant his motion to strike and allow him to file the attached responses.

Form: Requests for Production

To: [Party] through [attorney/address]

Under Rule 34, Federal Rules of Civil Procedure, produce for inspection the following documents and things:

[Set them out as specifically as possible.]

Form: Request for Medical Examination

Under Rule 35, Federal Rules of Civil Procedure, [party 1] asks the court to order [party 2] to submit to a [physical/mental/psychological, etc.] examination by [name\address of physician], as allowed by [rule].

1.   [Party 2's] [medical] condition is in controversy in this case and good cause exists for this relevant examination.

2.   Good cause exists because this examination is required for [party 1] to adequately prepare for trial.

Form: Request to Inspect Land

To: [Opposing parties and counsel]

[Party 1] asks permission for [name of party or nonparty] to permit [party 1] to enter [description of premises] as allowed by Rule 34, Federal Rules of Civil Procedure.

1.   It is necessary to [party 1's] trial preparation to enter the land to [inspect, measure, photograph, test, etc.].

2.   [Party 1] asks that [identity of persons to attend] be permitted to attend.

3.   [Party 1] asks that the inspection be made on [date/time].

4.   If permission is denied and [party 1] is required to file a motion, [party 1] will request sanctions, including attorney's fees.

Form: Motion for Protective Order

[Party 1] asks the court to protect it from [party 2's] request for [specific discovery request].

#.   A trial court has broad discretion to protect a party with a protective order. [Authority.] [Party1] asks the court to grant a protective order because it is necessary to protect [Party 1] from [state reason, which may include:

> undue burden
> unnecessary expense
> harassment
> invasion of privacy]

#.   [Party 1] requests a hearing and after hearing, that the court issue an order protecting [Party 1] from [the discovery] by [state requested action, which may include:

> denying {the requested discovery};
> limiting the extent of the subject matter to {state};
> sealing the discovery results;
> restricting the disclosure of the results to {list},

It would be a wonderful world to live in if all parties functioned properly and provided all requested discovery. But sometimes that doesn't happen, and you may need to ask the court to issue orders.

Form: Motion to Compel Discovery

#.   [Party 1] served [identify the discovery] on [party 2] on [date], under Rule [#], Texas Rules of Civil Procedure.

#.   [Party 1's] requested discovery is proper and within the scope of discovery permitted by the rules of procedure.

#.   [Party 2] has failed to respond within the required time.

#.   [Party 2's] noncompliance hinders [party 1's] discovery efforts and trial preparation and has caused [party 1] to incur additional attorney's fees in filing this motion.

[Party 1] asks to court to order [party 2] to respond to [party 1's] discovery requests and to pay [party 1] $xxx for expenses in filing this motion.

Jury Questions

Before going to appellate forms, I want to spend some time on jury questions and instructions. This is a part of any trial where the competent LA can be extremely valuable to the lawyer. It's an area often overlooked in reference books for LAs. I believe that is a mistake. One of the most important assets an LA can have is a thorough understanding of jury issues.

Sometimes the general topic of jury questions, instructions, and definitions is referred to as "the charge." It is really the general and special questions for the jury to answer and the instructions and definitions given for the jury to do that. We have all heard of cases that have been overturned because of the misplacement of a comma in a jury instruction; I worked on one such case when I was in St. Louis. A case I worked on in Houston resulted in a hung jury after a two-month trial and several days of jury deliberations, because they just didn't understand the charge. What a waste of time. In that case, the jury questions and instructions were all "standard," from form books and pattern jury charges. Go figure.

Preparing the jury questions is critical and calls for clear thinking, excellent research, and fortitude. Many times the jury questions are worked and reworked late at night, at the end of a long and exhausting trial. (This happens in spite of your having prepared proposed jury questions as part of the pretrial order before trial ever started.) People are not always at their best at such late hours during the stress of a trial.

Yet they must be if working on jury questions. If you have worked on the jury questions ahead of time, you are *hours* ahead when those long nights arrive.

Some of the best advice I ever got was from Joe Reynolds during one of my first trials with him. He is always well prepared (one of the marks of a great lawyer and befitting his status as a member of the American College Trial Lawyers and the "Best Lawyers in America"). That advice was to *"work backward from the jury questions. "*

If you can determine early in the case what the jury issues will be, you can always be working toward that in your proof. Your discovery will become meaningful rather than boilerplate. If you can get your lawyer to give some attention to the jury issues long before they are being dictated for the actual jury, you will score more wins than losses. More important, you will save countless hours.

There are form books of "pattern jury instructions" available in all states. You will also find federal pattern jury instructions for each of the 13 federal circuits. There are books with titles like *Court's Charge Reporter*, that will report jury charges from actual cases. Just as case law evolves, so do jury questions and instructions. They are based on our changing law, after all. And even though it is the lawyer who prepares them, it is vital that the LA understand this process.

Each judge probably will have already prepared all the general instructions. The attorneys will be able to offer special questions and instructions for the particular case. Each jury charge should be customized for the individual case. As to certain causes of action, every element must be satisfied, so jury instructions often include each of those elements. For instance, fraud, conspiracy, antitrust, 10(b)5 cases, and the like all have elements; if any are missing, the case has not been made.

When it's time in the trial for the jury instructions to be prepared, the attorneys usually meet with the judge in chambers for a "charge conference." The attorneys will ask that certain questions and instructions be given (slanted, of course, in their particular direction), offering authority for each. A record will be made of whether they are given, denied, or modified. The rulings can be the basis of an appeal.

If the LA has anticipated the lawyer's need for jury instructions and has something ready to work on, the benefit is incalculable. So here are some suggestions for your guidance—always with the admonition to be familiar with the rules and law for your particular jurisdiction. These jury questions are either from actual cases or are pattern instructions from the federal circuits. Not all of them are in plain language, but since they are from actual court cases, I have not disturbed them. You should know enough by this point in this book about unnecessary words. And you and your attorney can determine, according to the law in your jurisdiction, what words are not required.

Jury Charge for the Largest Verdict Ever

The largest verdict in history was in Houston (over $11 *billion*, including punitive damages), in a tortious interference case involving an "agreement to agree" and tried under both New York and Texas law. The winning trial team was headed by the famous King of Torts, Houston's Joe Jamail, who worked with Baker & Botts, a Houston "megafirm." The charge was based on what was then in Texas called "special issues" (now they're called "jury questions"), and there were only eight of them.

I thought you might be interested in the charge from that case, and I have included it here, verbatim (including grammatical errors), from the public record. The citation is *Texaco, Inc. v. Pennzoil Co.*, 729 S.W.2d 768 (Tex. App.—Houston [1st Dist.] 1987, writ ref'd n.r.e.), *cert. dism'd,* 108 S. Ct. 1305 (1988).

Sample: Charge of the Court in *Pennzoil Co. v. Texaco Inc.*

Members of the jury:

    This case is submitted to you on special issues consisting of specific questions about the facts, which you must decide from the evidence you have heard in this trial. You are the sole judges of the credibility of the witnesses and the weight to be given their testimony, but in matters of law, you must be governed by the instructions in this charge. In discharging your responsibility on this jury, you will observe all the instructions which have previously been given you. I shall now give you additional instructions which you should carefully and strictly follow during your deliberations.

    1. Do not let bias, prejudice or sympathy play any part in your deliberations.

    2. In arriving at your answers, consider only the evidence introduced here under oath and such exhibits, if any, as have been introduced for your consideration under the rulings of the Court, that is, what you have seen and heard in this courtroom, together with the law as given you by the court. In your deliberations, you will not consider or discuss anything that is not represented by the evidence in this case.

    3. Since every answer that is required by the charge is important, no juror should state or consider that any required answer is not important.

    4. You must not decide who you think should win, and then try to answer the questions accordingly. Simply answer the questions, and do not discuss nor concern yourselves with the effect of your answers.

    5. You will not decide an issue by lot or by drawing straws, or by any other method of chance. Do not return a quotient verdict. A quotient verdict means that the jurors agree to abide by the result to be reached by adding together each juror's figure and dividing by the number of jurors to get an average. Do not do any trading on your answers; that is, one juror should not agree to answer a certain question one way if others will agree to answer another question another way.

6.   You may render your verdict upon the vote of ten or more members of the jury. The same ten or more of you must agree upon all of the answers made and to the entire verdict. You will not, therefore, enter into an agreement to be bound by a majority or any other vote of less than ten jurors. If the verdict and all of the answers therein are reach by unanimous agreement, the presiding juror shall sign the verdict for the entire jury. If any juror disagrees as to any answer made by the verdict, those jurors who agree to all findings shall each sign the verdict.

These instructions are given you because your conduct is subject to review the same as that of the witnesses, parties, attorneys and the judge. If it should be found that you have disregarded any of these instructions, it will be jury misconduct and it may require another trial by another jury; then all of our time will have been wasted.

The presiding juror or any other juror who observes a violation of the court's instructions shall immediately warn the one who is violating the same and caution the juror not to do so again.

When words are used in this Charge in a sense which varies from the meaning commonly understood, you are given a proper legal definition which you are bound to accept in place of any other definition or meaning.

The Court now gives you such definitions of terms or words used in the Charge.

By the term "preponderance of the evidence" as used in this Charge, is meant the greater weight and degree of credible evidence before you.

SPECIAL ISSUE No. 1

Do you find from a preponderance of the evidence that at the end of the Getty Oil board meeting of January 3, 1984, Pennzoil and each of the Getty entities, to wit, the Getty Oil Company, the Sarah C.

Getty Trust and the J. Paul Getty Museum, intended to bind themselves to an agreement that included the following terms:

a. *all Getty Oil shareholders except Pennzoil and the Sarah C. Getty Trust were to receive $110 per share, plus the right to receive a deferred cash consideration from the sale of ERC Corporation of at least $5 per share within five years;*

b. *Pennzoil was to own 3/7ths of the stock of Getty Oil and the Sarah C. Getty Trust was to own the remaining 4/7ths of the stock of Getty Oil; and*

c. *Pennzoil and the Sarah C. Getty Trust were to endeavor in good faith to agree upon a plan for restructuring Getty Oil on or before December 31, 1984, and if they were unable to reach such agreement then they would divide the assets of Getty Oil between them also on a 3/7ths - 4/7ths basis*

Answer: "We do" or "We do not." _____

INSTRUCTIONS

1. *An agreement may be oral, it may be written or it may be partly written and partly oral. Where an agreement is fully or partially in writing, the law provides that persons may bind themselves to that agreement even though they do not sign it, where their assent is otherwise indicated.*

2. *In answering Issue No. 1, you should look to the intent of Pennzoil and the Getty entities as outwardly or objectively demonstrated to each other by their words and deeds. The question is not determined by the parties' secret, inward, or subjective intentions.*

3. *Persons may intend to be bound to an agreement even though they plan to sign a more formal and detailed document at a later time. On the other hand, parties may intend not to be bound until such a document is signed.*

4. *There is no legal requirement that parties agree on all the matters incidental to their agreement before they can intend to*

be bound. Thus, even if certain matters were left for future negotiations, those matters may not have been regarded by Pennzoil and the Getty entities as essential to their agreement, if any, on January 3. On the other hand, you may find that the parties did not intend to be bound until each and every term of their transaction was resolved.

5. *Every binding agreement carries with it a duty of good faith performance. If Pennzoil and the Getty entities intended to be bound at the end of the Getty Oil board meeting on January 3, they were obliged to negotiate in good faith the terms of the definitive merger agreement and to carry out the transaction.*

6. *Modification or discussions to modify an agreement do not defeat or nullify a prior intention to be bound. Parties may always, by mutual consent and understanding, add new provisions spelling out additional terms that were not included in their original agreement.*

SPECIAL ISSUE NO. 2

Do you find from a preponderance of the evidence that Texaco knowingly interfered with the agreement between Pennzoil and the Getty entities, if you have so found?

Answer: "We do" or "We do not."

ANSWER: _____

1. *Knowledge of a fact can be shown either by direct evidence of what it knew or what it was told, or by indirect or circumstantial evidence. A fact may be established by indirect or circumstantial evidence when the fact is fairly and reasonably inferred from other facts proven in the case. In order to find that Texaco interfered with the agreement, if any, inquired about above, it must be shown by a preponderance of the evidence that Texaco wanted to cause the breach, or to prevent the performance of this agreement, or that Texaco*

knew that a breach or failure to perform would occur as a result of its actions.

2. *In order to find that Texaco had knowledge of the agreement, if any, it is not necessary that Texaco had an accurate understanding of the legal significance of the facts which produced the agreement. If Texaco knew the facts that gave rise to the agreement, then it knew of the agreement, even if it did not believe that those facts gave rise to an agreement and even if it believed that any agreement that did exist violated the law. You may also find that Texaco knew of the agreement, if any, if you find that Texaco intentionally or willfully refused to ascertain the facts or if it exercised bad faith. Texaco is also charged with all the knowledge, if any, of its agents and representatives, whether communicated to each other or not.*

3. *A party may interfere with an agreement by persuasion alone, by offering better terms, by giving an indemnity against damage claims to the party or parties induced to breach, or any act interfering with the performance of a legal duty arising from the agreement, such as the duty of good faith performance.*

4. *A competitor has no privilege and is not permitted to interfere with the agreements of those with whom it is in competition. Also, a party is not justified in interfering with the agreement of another simply because it is advancing its own business interests.*

5. *You may find that Texaco knowingly interfered with the Pennzoil agreement, if any, even though the Getty Oil directors, the Museum's President, and Gordon P. Getty, Trustee, were fiduciaries. If those fiduciaries showed an intention to be bound to an agreement with Pennzoil on January 3, they could not avoid that agreement by later seeking or accepting a higher price or a more beneficial arrangement with a third party.*

SPECIAL ISSUE NO. 3

What sum of money, if any, do you find from a preponderance of the evidence would compensate Pennzoil for its actual damages, if any, suffered as a direct and natural result of Texaco's knowingly interfering with the agreement between Pennzoil and the Getty entities, if any?

Answer in dollars and cents.

ANSWER: $_____

1. *The measure of damages in this case is the amount necessary to put Pennzoil in as good a position as it would have had if its agreement with the Getty entities, if any, had been performed.*

2. *Pennzoil must prove its damages, if any, with a reasonable degree of certainty. This does not, however, require proof to an absolute mathematical certainty. If a wrong has been done from which monetary loss results, you may make a just and reasonable estimate of the damage based on relevant data, including opinion evidence, even if the extent of injury cannot be proven precisely. Damages cannot be remote or contingent.*

SPECIAL ISSUE NO. 4

Do you find from a preponderance of the evidence that Texaco's actions, if any, were intentional, willful and in wanton disregard of the rights of Pennzoil, if any?

Answer: _____ ("We do" or We do not")

If and only if you have answered Special Issue No. 4 "We do", then you are to answer Special Issue No. 5.

SPECIAL ISSUE NO. 5

What sum of money, if any, is Pennzoil entitled to receive from Texaco as punitive damages?

Answer in dollars and cents.

ANSWER: $_____

Punitive damages means an amount that you may in your discretion award as an example to others and as a penalty or by way of punishment, in addition to any amount you may have found as actual damages.

It is not necessary to show that Texaco was motivated by ill will or hatred of Pennzoil.

In assessing punitive damages, if any, you may take into account not merely the act or acts of Texaco itself. You may also take into account all the circumstances, including Texaco's motives and the extent of damages, if any, suffered by Pennzoil.

SPECIAL ISSUE NO. 6

Do you find from a preponderance of the evidence that at the end of the Getty Oil Company Board meeting on January 3, 1984, the Getty Oil Company, the Museum, the Trust, and Pennzoil each intended to be bound to an agreement which provided that the Getty Oil Company would purchase the Museum shares forthwith as provided in the "Memorandum of Agreement"?

Answer "We do" or "We do not."

ANSWER: _____

SPECIAL ISSUE NO. 7

Do you find from a preponderance of the evidence that at the end of the Getty Oil Company Board meeting on January 3, 1984, the

Getty Oil Company, the Museum, the Trust, and Pennzoil each intended to be bound to an agreement which provided for Pennzoil to have an option to purchase 8 million shares of Getty Oil Company stock as provided in the "Memorandum of Agreement"?

Answer "We do" or "We do not."

ANSWER: _____

SPECIAL ISSUE NO. 8

Do you find from a preponderance of the evidence that the payment of $110 in cash per share plus the ERC stub was not a fair price?

Answer "It was not a fair price" or "It was a fair price"

ANSWER: _____

You are instructed that a "fair price" is a price reached between a willing buyer who is not required to buy and a willing seller, who is under no obligation to sell.

After you retire to the jury room, you will select your own presiding juror. The first thing the presiding juror will do is to have this complete charge read aloud and then you will deliberate upon your answers to the questions asked.

It is the duty of the presiding juror:

1. *to preside during your deliberations;*

2. *to see that your deliberations are conducted in an orderly manner and in accordance with the instructions in this charge;*

3. *to write out and hand to the bailiff any communication concerning the case which you desire to have delivered to the judge;*

4. *to conduct the vote on the issues and participate in that vote;*

5. *to write your answers to the issues in the spaces provided; and*

6. *to certify to your verdict in the space provided for the presiding juror's signature or to obtain the signatures of all the jurors who agree with the verdict if your verdict is less than unanimous.*

After you have retired to consider your verdict, no one has any authority to communicate with you except the bailiff of this Court. You should not discuss the case with anyone, not even with other members of the jury, unless all of you are present and assembled in the jury room. Should anyone attempt to talk to you about the case before the verdict is returned, whether at the courthouse, at your home, or elsewhere, please inform the judge of this fact.

When you have answered all of the questions which you are required to answer under the instructions of the judge, and your foreman has placed your answers in the spaces provided, and signed the verdict as foreman or obtain the signatures, you will advise the bailiff at the door of the jury room that you have reached a verdict, and then you will return into Court with your verdict.

_____
Judge Presiding

CERTIFICATE

We the jury, have answered the above and foregoing special issues as herein indicated, and herewith return same into court as our verdict.

(To be signed by the presiding juror if unanimous)

_____

Presiding Juror

To be signed by those rendering the verdict if not unanimous.

_____   _____

_____   _____

_____   _____

_____   _____

_____   _____

_____

Notice that issue 5 in the *Pennzoil* case is a "conditional" one. It is conditioned on a finding in another question. Any jury question that begins with words like "if you have found" is referred to as a conditional question.

A recent innovation in jury trials is that of the "dynamite" charge. That is a supplemental charge given to a jury that appears to be hung, or in danger of hanging by virtue of the time it has been spent in deliberations without reaching a verdict. The judge will call the jury back into the courtroom and read them the supplemental charge. Sometimes the call for a "dynamite" charge may be backed by a sense of panic and you can provide a great service if you already have one at your fingertips.

Form: Dynamite charge

SUPPLEMENTAL CHARGE

Members of the jury:

You are instructed that in a large proportion of cases, absolute certainty cannot be expected; although the verdict must be the verdict of each individual juror, and not a mere acquiescence in the conclusion of other jurors, yet each juror should examine the Court's Charge with candor and with a proper regard and deference to each other.

It is your duty, as jurors, to consult with one another and to deliberate with a view to reaching an agreement, if you can do so without violence to individual judgment. Each of you must decide the case for yourself, but do so only after an impartial consideration of the evidence with your fellow jurors. In the course of your deliberations, do not hesitate to reexamine your own views and change your opinion if convinced it is erroneous. But do not surrender your honest conviction as to the weight or effect of evidence solely because of the opinion of your fellow jurors, or for the mere purpose of returning a verdict.

As you know, this is an important case, and the trial has been expensive both to the plaintiff and to the defendant. If you fail to agree on a verdict, the case is left open and undecided. You should consider that the case at some time must be decided, and that you 12 are selected in the same manner and from the same source from which each future jury must be, and there is no reason on the part of anyone to suppose that the case will ever be submitted to a jury more intelligent and more impartial or more competent to decide it or that more or clearer evidence will be produced on one side or the other.

Please continue your deliberations in an effort to reach a verdict.

_____

Presiding Judge

So that's an example of an entire jury charge, as given by the judge aloud to the jury. The jury then takes that charge and verdict form to the jury room for their deliberations.

And here are some forms from some of the more common types of cases.

Form: Independent Contractor Definition

An independent contractor is a person who performs services for another person under an express or implied agreement and who is not subject to the other's control, or right to control, the manner and means of performing the services.

One who engages an independent contractor is not liable to others for the acts or omissions of the independent contractor.

Form: Corporation's Liability Instruction

All persons are equal before the law and a [corporation] [partnership] is entitled to the same fair and conscientious consideration by you as any other person.

Under the law, a corporation is a person. It can act only through its employees, agents, directors, or officers. Therefore, a corporation is responsible for the acts of its employees, agents, directors, and officers performed within the scope of authority.

Forms: General Partnership Definitions and Instructions

A partnership is an association of two or more persons to carry on a business as co-owners. The members of a partnership are called partners.

A partner is acting within the scope of the partnership business when doing anything which is either expressly or impliedly authorized by the partnership or which is in furtherance of partnership business.

An act or omission of a partner within the scope of the partnership business is the act or omission of all partners.

A partnership can act only through its employees, agents, or partners. Therefore, a partnership is responsible for the acts of its employees, agents, and partners performed within the scope of authority.

The defendants [names] are partners. [Name of partner] was acting on behalf of the partnership and within the scope of authority. Therefore, if you decide for the plaintiff, your verdict must be against all of the partners.

-or-

It is denied that [acting partner] was acting within the scope of the partnership business.

If [acting partner] was acting within the scope of the partnership business, and if you find against [acting partner], then you must find against [both] [all] defendants.

If you find for [acting partner], then you must find for [both][all] defendants.

If you find against [acting partner], but you do not find that [acting partner] was acting within the scope of the partnership business, then you must find for the defendant [nonacting partner].

Forms: Agency Definitions and Instructions

An agent is a person who performs services for another person under an express or implied agreement and who is subject to the other's control or right to control the manner and means of performing the services. The other person is called a principal.

One may be an agent without receiving compensation for services.

The agency agreement may be oral or written.

An agent is acting within the scope of authority if the agent is engaged in the performance of duties which were expressly or impliedly assigned to the agent by the principal.

Any act or omission of an agent within the scope of authority is the act or omission of the principal.

The defendants are sued as principal and agent. The defendant [principal's name] is the principal and the defendant [agent's name] is the agent. If you find against [agent's name], then you must also find against [principal's name]. However, if you find for [agent's name], then you must also find for [principal's name].

Form: Fraud Jury Instructions

Fraud occurs when a false representation of material fact is made with intent to induce the listener to act upon it and the listener acts in reliance upon the misrepresentation and suffers injury as a consequence.

The elements of actionable fraud are:

1. That a material misrepresentation was made;

2. That it was false;

3. That, when the speaker made it, he knew it was false or made it recklessly without any knowledge of its truth and as a positive assertion;

4. That he made it with the intention that the party act on it;

5. That the party acted in reliance on it; and

6. That the party suffered injury as a result of the reliance.

A promise to do an act in the future is actionable fraud when made with the intention, purpose, and design of deceiving, and with no intention of performing the act.

A "misrepresentation" may consist of the concealment of a material fact when there is a duty to speak. The duty to speak or to disclose arises when one party knows that the other party is relying on the concealed fact, provided that he knows the relying party is ignorant of the facts and does not have an equal opportunity to discover the truth.

You are further instructed that if during the course of dealings between the parties a representation was true when made, the party making the representation may not remain silent after the party learns that the representation is no longer true. In such a case, and in order to find fraud, you must additionally find that the party did not use reasonable or ordinary care to disclose to the other party, before the transaction was consummated, any subsequently acquired information which the party recognizes as making untrue or misleading a previous representation.

Form: Fraud Jury Questions

Was [name] induced to sign the [date] note by the fraud, if any, of [bank]?

Do you find that the representation, if any, of [company], through its officers, agents, or employees, that it would not compete with [company] in the sale of [product] constituted fraud?

Form: Jury Question and Instruction on Estoppel

Do you find that [party] is estopped to deny the agreement?

Answer "yes" or "no."

ANSWER: _____

You are instructed that in order for a party to be "estopped," you must find that the party to be estopped has made

1. A false representation or concealment of material facts;

2. With knowledge, actual or constructive, of the facts;

3. To a party without knowledge, or the means of acquiring knowledge of the facts;

4. With the intention that the representation or concealment be acted on; and

5. The party to whom the representation was made or facts concealed from must have reasonably relied or acted on the representation or concealment to that party's prejudice.

Form: Civil Conspiracy Jury Questions and Instructions

Do you find that on [date] there existed a civil conspiracy between any of the following parties to deprive [party] of [or whatever the allegation is]?

Answer "we do" or "we do not" as to each party:

Answer: [party's name]   _____

Answer: [party's name]   _____

Answer: [party's name]   _____

You are instructed that a civil conspiracy is an agreement or understanding on the part of two or more persons (which includes corporations) either to accomplish an unlawful purpose or to accomplish a lawful purpose by unlawful means. In order to find the existence of a civil conspiracy, you must find:

1. That there was a combination of two or more persons or entities;

2. That there was an agreement or meeting of the minds among those persons or entities for a common purpose;

3. That each of those persons or entities had knowledge of the purpose;

4. That each of those persons or entities intended to participate therein;

5. That there was an intent to inflict injury; and

6. That one or more acts were done in furtherance of the civil conspiracy.

The elements of a civil conspiracy may, therefore, be provided by direct or circumstantial evidence as well as by the acts or declarations of the conspirators touching on their intended or accomplished purposes. Moreover, a civil conspiracy may be established by proof showing concert to action or other facts or circumstances from which the reasonable and natural inference arises that the acts were committed in the furtherance of the common design, intention, or purpose of the conspiracy.

Further, it is not required that each and every act of a conspirator be shown to have been in concert with others or that it be established by direct proof that all the conspirators combined at a given time prior to each act or transaction. Therefore, it is not necessary to prove that each of the conspirators was present at each act or transaction which forms the basis of the civil conspiracy. Moreover, persons may enter into the civil conspiracy at different times. All parties to a civil conspiracy are responsible for each and every act of any conspirator carrying out the civil conspiracy.

You are instructed that in determining whether a conspiracy existed you should consider the actions and declarations of all the alleged conspirators. However, in determining whether a particular party was a member of the conspiracy, if any, you should consider only his acts and statements. He cannot be bound by the acts or declarations of the alleged coconspirators until it is established that a conspiracy existed, that he was one of its members, and that the act or declaration was made during the course of and in furtherance of the conspiracy.

LAs, I submit that if those who draft pleadings would study what the jury instructions are for a particular cause of action, they might not make unfounded allegations. As you can see from these instructions, conspiracy is very difficult to prove.

I once worked on a civil conspiracy case where the judge had trouble with the word "unlawful" in a jury charge for a civil conspiracy rather than a criminal one. She asked the lawyers to work on drafting a conspiracy instruction that did not include the word "unlawful." That was a pretty difficult task, because nearly every jury question you find on civil conspiracy contains that word. But we did it, and, in case you ever have a need for it, here is what was given to the jury:

> *Did any of the following persons conspire to deny [name] his right to require the corporation to buy back his stock?*
>
> *"Conspiracy" is an agreement or understanding between two or more persons regarding an intended result. There must be a preconceived plan and a common design or purpose.*

Form: Willful/Malicious Jury Instruction

"Willfully and maliciously" means the intentional doing of a wrongful act without just cause or excuse for believing it to be right or legal, or done with conscious disregard to the rights of others. Willfulness and intent may be inferred by the actions and conduct of the wrongdoer.

Form: Damage Jury Question

What sum of money, if any, if paid now in cash do you find from a preponderance of the evidence would fairly and reasonably compensate [party] for his damage, if any, proximately caused by [party's negligence, fraud, civil conspiracy, etc.]? [This question would be conditioned on the finding of negligence, etc.]

Answer in dollars and cents, if any.

Answer: $_____

Form: Damage Jury Instruction

If you find for the [plaintiff], you must determine [plaintiff's] damages. [Plaintiff] has the burden of proving damages by a preponderance of the evidence. Damages means the amount of money which will reasonably and fairly compensate the plaintiff for any [injury] [and] [or] [property damage] you find was [proximately] [legally] caused by the [negligence, whatever] of the defendant. You should consider the following [select as appropriate]:

The nature and extent of the injuries

The [disability] [disfigurement] [loss of enjoyment of life] experienced [and which with reasonable probability will be experienced in the future]

The [mental], [physical], [emotional] pain and suffering experienced [and which with reasonable probability will be experienced in the future]

The reasonable value of necessary medical care, treatment, and services received to the present time

The reasonable value of necessary medical care, treatment, and services which with reasonable probability will be required in the future

The reasonable value of [wages] [earnings] [earning capacity] [salaries] [employment] [business opportunities] [employment opportunities] lost to the present time

The reasonable value of [wages] [earnings] [earning capacity] [salaries] [employment] [business opportunities] [employment opportunities] which with reasonable probability will be lost in the future

The reasonable value of necessary repairs to any property which was damaged

The difference between the fair market value of any damaged property immediately before the occurrence and its fair market value immediately thereafter

The reasonable value of necessary repairs to any property that was damaged plus the difference between the fair market value of the property immediately before the occurrence and its fair market value after it was repaired

The lesser of the following:

The reasonable cost of necessary repairs to any property that was damaged plus the difference between the fair market value of the property immediately before the occurrence and its fair market value after repair;

or

The difference between the fair market value of the property immediately before the occurrence and the fair market value of the unrepaired property immediately after the occurrence.

Such sum as will reasonably compensate for any loss of use of any damaged property during the time reasonably required for its [repair] [replacement].

You may award damages for any bodily injury that the plaintiff sustained and any pain and suffering, [disability], [disfigurement], [mental anguish], [loss of capacity to enjoy life] that the plaintiff experienced in the past [or will experience in the future] as a result of the bodily injury. No evidence of the value of intangible things, such as mental or physical pain and suffering, has been or need be introduced. You are not trying to determine value, but an amount that will fairly compensate the plaintiff for the damages he has suffered. There is no exact standard for fixing the compensation to be awarded for these elements of damage. Any award you make should be fair in the light of the evidence.

You may award damages for aggravation of an existing disease or physical defect [or activation of any such latent condition] resulting from physical injury to the plaintiff. If you find that there was such an aggravation, you should determine, if you can, what portion of the plaintiff's condition resulted from the aggravation, and make allowance in your verdict only for the aggravation.

Any past [and future] loss of [his][her] spouse's services, comfort, society, and attention that the plaintiff has suffered [and will suffer] because of [his][her] spouse's injury.

Any loss of [his, her, their] child's services and earnings [or earning capacity] that the plaintiff has sustained in the past [and will sustain in the future, until the child reaches majority] because of the child's injury.

Form: Multiple Defendants/Claims Damages Jury Instructions

You must not award compensatory damages more than once for the same injury. For example, if the plaintiff prevails on two claims and establishes a dollar amount for his injuries, you must not award him any additional compensatory damages on each claim. The plaintiff is entitled to be made whole only once and may not recover more than he has lost. Of course, if different injuries are attributed to the separate claims, then you must compensate the plaintiff fully for all of his injuries.

With respect to punitive damages, you may make separate awards on each claim that plaintiff has established.

You may impose damages on a claim solely upon the defendant or defendants that you find are liable on that claim. Although there are [number] defendants in this case, it does not necessarily follow that if one is liable, all or any of the others also are liable. Each defendant is entitled to fair, separate, and individual consideration of his case without regard to your decision as to the other defendants. If you find that only one defendant is responsible for a particular injury, then you must award damages for that injury against only that defendant.

Form: Exemplary Damages Jury Instruction

Exemplary damages are sums of money assessed, in such amounts as are appropriate under the facts, as a warning and as an example to prevent others from committing like offenses and wrongs. You may take into consideration the losses of [party], if any, not otherwise compensable, such as compensation for inconvenience and expense of litigation and loss of business. Other factors to be used in determining the amount of exemplary damages, if any, include the nature of the wrong, the character of conduct involved, the degree of culpability, the situation and sensibilities of the parties concerned and the extent to which such conduct offends public sense of justice and propriety.

Answer separately as to each applicable defendant, if any.
Answer in dollars and cents, if any.

ANSWER:

[Party] $_____

[Party] $_____

[Party] $_____

[Party] $_____

Form: Punitive Damages Jury Instruction

If you find that the defendant is liable for the plaintiff's injuries, you must award the plaintiff the compensatory damages that he has proven. You also may award punitive damages, if the plaintiff has proved that the defendant acted with malice or willfulness or with callous and reckless indifference to the safety or rights of others. One acts willfully or with reckless indifference to the rights of others when he acts in disregard of a high and excessive degree of danger about which he knows or which would be apparent to a reasonable person in his condition.

If you determine that the defendant's conduct was so shocking and offensive as to justify an award of punitive damages, you may exercise your discretion to award those damages. In making any award of punitive damages, you should consider that the purpose of punitive damages is to punish a defendant for shocking conduct, and to deter the defendant and others from engaging in similar conduct in the future. The law does not require you to award punitive damages; however, if you decide to award punitive damages, you must use sound reason in setting the amount of the damages. The amount of an award of punitive damages must not reflect bias, prejudice, or sympathy toward any party. However, the amount can be as large as you believe necessary to fulfill the purposes of punitive damages. You may consider the financial resources of the defendant in fixing the amount of punitive damages [and you may impose punitive damages against one or more of the defendants, and not others, or against more than one defendant in different amounts].

Form: Damages Instruction—Mitigation

The plaintiff has a duty to use reasonable efforts to mitigate damages. To mitigate means to avoid or reduce damages.

The defendant has the burden of proving by a preponderance of the evidence:

1. That plaintiff failed to use reasonable efforts to mitigate damages; and

2. The amount by which damages would have been mitigated.

D. Appellate Forms

Tips:

The notice of appeal and requests for record inclusions are filed in the trial court. All subsequent documents, including requests for continuance, are filed in the appellate court.

Check the rules for page limits, prescribed format, color of covers of briefs, and other requisites.

Calendar all deadlines, on more than one calendar. Enter deadlines into the docket control system. Under most systems, all times will run from the signing of the judgment.

An appeal is the way in which a party can challenge a judgment or order. The appeals court does not try the case—it merely reviews the lower court's decision to ensure that no errors were made.

The first step in preparing for an appeal is to determine to which court you are appealing. The LA has great responsibilities in the preparation of an appeal: Organizational skills and knowledge of the appellate rules and deadlines will help keep your attorney on the right track.

As already mentioned, computation of time is critical, and it is especially critical in appellate matters. Even though you do occasionally get some leeway, depending on the court, you don't want to lose a case because you didn't get your brief or record filed timely. Since I haven't yet discussed computing time, here is a refresher for you.

In computing time, the day of the act, event, or default from which the designated period of time begins to run is *not* included. The last day of the period *is* included, unless it is a Saturday, Sunday, or legal holiday, and then the period runs until the end of the next day. Fed. R. App. P. 26(a).

For example, if the judgment is signed on July 10, the first day of the period is July 11. Your deadline for filing a motion for new trial would be July 20, the tenth day after judgment is signed. The notice of appeal is due in 30 days, or August 9. Fed. R. App. P. 4(a)(4).

The clerk of the trial court prepares the record as to pertinent documents. Appellant must order transcript of testimony, which completes the appellate record, from the court reporter within ten days of filing the notice of appeal. Generally, that request will include a cash deposit. Depending on the length of trial, the transcript of testimony can be very long, and thus, expensive. The record is due to be filed with the court within 30 days of court reporter's receipt of the request. Fed. R. App. P. 11. You will need to follow up with the reporter to determine if an extension of time is needed because the court reporter hasn't completed the transcription of the trial testimony.

Appellant's brief is due 40 days after the record is filed; appellee's brief is due 30 days after appellant's brief is filed; appellant's reply brief is due 14 days after appellee's brief is filed. Fed. R. App. P. 31(a).

Except for briefs and appendices, papers will *not* be timely unless they are *actually received* by the clerk within the time fixed for filing. Briefs and appendices are deemed filed on the day of mailing if the most expeditious form of delivery by mail is used. Fed. R. App. P. 26(c).

Tip:

Be sure to check with the *proper* clerk of the *proper* court in determining whether the courthouse is closed. For example, in *Seismic & Digital Concepts, Inc. v. Digital Resources Corp.*, 583 S.W.2d 442 (Tex. Civ. App.--Houston [1st Dist.] 1979, no writ), the lawyer relied on incorrect information given to him by the county courthouse switchboard operator that the courthouse would be closed because of a holiday when, in fact, the court of appeals was open for business. Relying on this misinformation [and failing to double-check with the clerk of the court of appeals] the appellant failed to timely file a motion to extend the deadline for filing the statement of facts (transcript of testimony).

Courts require timely filing of all papers within the period of time allowed by the rules. Fed. R. App. P. 26. Extensions of time for filing documents are looked upon with disfavor; however, the fifth circuit will frequently grant an extension of time to file the brief, and most other circuits probably will as well, provided there is no abuse. In the fifth circuit, no motion is required—simply call the clerk and request additional time.

The LA can easily handle this task and then follow up the conversation with a letter to the clerk confirming the granted extension and the amended deadline, and provide copies to all interested parties. In Texas appellate courts, a written motion is required and it must be verified. And you may not have more than three extensions of time.

I can't emphasize too strongly; check the rules of the court you're in. Know where the rules are and check them many times. Don't trust your memory. Knowing the rules of procedure should be one of the really strong attributes of the competent LA. The lawyer shouldn't have to spend too much time on keeping up with rule changes if the LA assisting him is competent. Make a timetable chart and note changes when the rules of procedure are amended.

A few words about cover colors. The federal appellate courts and the United States Supreme Court have rules about colors of covers of briefs: Appellant's brief in light blue; appellee's brief in red; reply briefs gray; briefs of amicus curiae green. Texas appellate courts do not have rules for cover colors, but most lawyers follow the federal rules. However, one of our appellate courts in Houston has only one color rule: *Anything but red!* Print doesn't show up very well on red cover stock. So how do we handle it? Many ways. We use pink for appellee's brief, or we use clear covers with red backing and binding.

A word about binding. Please use spiral binding. It will lie flat while the law clerks and judges read the brief. Make it easy for them.

Here is an outline of a brief for appellant in our state court. It will be just about the same if you are in federal court, but check the rules.

Form: Appellant's Brief

NO. C14-96-0195-CV

IN THE COURT OF APPEALS

FOR THE FOURTEENTH SUPREME JUDICIAL DISTRICT

AT HOUSTON, TEXAS

DAVID GOODBODY and THOMAS YOUNGSTER,
ASSIGNEES OF GARTH SIMPSON,

Appellants

V.

MICHAEL FREEMAN and HARRY GRAND,

Appellees

BRIEF OF APPELLANTS,
DAVID GOODBODY and THOMAS YOUNGSTER,
ASSIGNEES OF GARTH SIMPSON

Charles Porter, 15555555   George A. Bennett, 02223033
1966 Oak Blvd, #920   BENNETT & BENNETT
Houston, TX 77000   1000 State Street
(713) 666-4444 fax 666-4445   Houston, Texas 77000-0000
                                  (713) 555-9797 fax 555-9798

Attorneys for Appellants
David Goodbody & Thomas Youngster,
Assignees of Garth Simpson

ORAL ARGUMENT REQUESTED

[Date]

[New Page]

TABLE OF CONTENTS

[new page]

INDEX OF AUTHORITIES

<u>Cases</u> <u>Page</u>

[List the cases alphabetically, without pinpoint cites]

<u>Constitutions, Statutes, Rules of Procedure</u>

<u>Secondary Authorities</u>

[New page]

NO. C14-96-0195-CV

IN THE COURT OF APPEALS

FOR THE FOURTEENTH SUPREME JUDICIAL DISTRICT

AT HOUSTON, TEXAS

DAVID GOODBODY AND THOMAS YOUNGSTER,
ASSIGNEES OF GARTH SIMPSON,

Appellants

V.

MICHAEL FREEMAN AND HARRY GRAND,

Appellees

BRIEF OF APPELLANTS
DAVID GOODBODY and THOMAS YOUNGSTER,
ASSIGNEES OF GARTH SIMPSON

Appellants David Goodbody and Thomas Youngster, assignees of
Garth Simpson ("Goodbody & Youngster"), file this their brief and state:

[New page]

Certificate of Interested Parties

[List all parties and all counsel.]

[The purpose is so that each member of the panel can decide if he should recuse himself.]

[New page]

Jurisdictional Statement

[Short and concise; try to do in one paragraph]

[New page]

Appellants' Points of Error

Point of Error 1

Point of Error 2

Point of Error 3

[continue through all points of error]

[New page]

Appellants' Statement of Facts

[Short and concise; try to do it in less than a page]

[At the federal level, this is the
Statement of Issues Presented for Review
and Statement of the Case]

[Include record references for each statement]

[New page]

BRIEF OF THE ARGUMENT

Point of Error 1
(restated)
**Argument and Authorities
Under Point of Error 1**

Point of Error 2
(restated)
**Argument and Authorities
Under Point of Error 2**

Point of Error 3
(restated)
**Argument and Authorities
Under Point of Error 3**

[continue through all points of error]

CONCLUSION

[keep it short, just a few sentences]

PRAYER FOR RELIEF

[Signature block]

CERTIFICATE OF SERVICE

I certify under [rule] that a copy of this brief has been served by mail on [date] on the following attorneys of record:

[LIST THEM WITH ALL INFORMATION, INCLUDING NAME OF PARTY REPRESENTED]

_____
George Bennett

Appellee's Brief and Other Considerations

Appellee's brief *responds* to appellant's brief, correcting any misstatements of fact. It will be formatted like appellant's brief, with a few differences. For example, if there are errors or misstatements in appellant's statements of fact, appellee will want to furnish his own statement of facts. Instead of points of error, there will be responses to appellant's points of error, or there may be cross-points of error.

Twenty-five copies of each brief must be filed with the clerk. Fed. R. App. P. 31(b). Always check your local rules to confirm the number

of copies required to be filed. The fifth circuit local rule 31.1 requires
seven copies of the briefs to be filed.

As of this writing, appellant's and appellee's brief must not exceed
50 pages, and reply briefs must not exceed 25 pages. The Table of Contents, Table of Authorities, and any addenda are not included in the page
count. Fed. R. App. P. 28(g). However, as noted earlier in this book,
rules are proposed to change the limits to *word limits*, rather than page
limits.

Under Federal Rule of Appellate Procedure 30(a), appellant must
prepare and file an appendix to the brief, including:

1. The relevant docket entries in the proceeding below

2. Any relevant portions of the pleadings, charge, findings, or
    opinion

3. The judgment, order, or decision being appealed

4. Any other parts of the record to which the parties wish to direct
    particular attention.

The rules encourage the parties to agree on the contents of the
appendix. Within 10 days after filing of the record, the appellant must
serve on the appellee a designation of the parts of the record which
appellant intends to include in the appendix and a statement of the issues
which the appellant intends to present for review. If appellee wishes to
include other parts of the record, he should serve a designation of those
parts on the appellant within 10 days of his receipt of the appellant's
designation. Fed. R. App. P. 30(b).

E. Miscellaneous Forms

Form: Outline of Trial Notebook

The LA is usually called on to prepare a trial notebook. This may be one binder or a box full of binders, depending on the case. I once saw a lawyer whose trial notebook was a cardboard box marked "trial notebook." (It worked for him.) The trial notebook is peculiar to a particular case, but there are areas common to all trial notebooks.

Some lawyers begin preparing their trial notebook as soon as they start work on the case. Others wait until it is pretty certain that the case will go to trial, and then they prepare it. A trial notebook is very useful to the trial lawyer in organizing his thoughts, his strategy, his witnesses, and his trial exhibits. There are several reasons for preparing a trial notebook:

Organizes everything in the trial

Makes it easy to find things—no fumbling before the jury

Enables senior litigators to review the work before trial

Makes it easy for someone else to take over if necessary

Gets the mental processes working and focused

Notes about the actual physical notebook:

Three-ring binder for 8 1/2" x 11" sheets is best

Consider silent slide fasteners
(those loud snaps and pops are distracting in a trial)

But: Some attorneys believe the "snap" produces a fearful anticipation in the opponent

Pockets are available for documents that are not to be hole-punched

You will probably need more than one binder

Contents of the Trial Notebook

Table of Contents

Preliminary draft first, to show what needs to be done as preparation progresses; final version is written last. Refer to sections rather than pages. Things go in and out of a trial notebook continually, so page numbering is impossible.

Analysis of the Case

The trial attorney's theory of the case; attorney's notes for the battle plan, including thoughts about voir dire, final argument, and jury questions.

Analysis of the Opponent's Case

What are the opponent's weaknesses? Strengths? Who are their best and worst witnesses? What witnesses do we use to counterattack their strong points?

Evidence

Checklist
Elements of the cause of action or defense
Evidence supporting each element
Source of the evidence

The checklist forces to you to cover every facet of the case. If there are any gaps, they will show up here. Helps grasp the totality of the evidence to refine the theory of the case. Refreshes the attorney's recollection about the case. Puts the evidence in perspective as the trial unfolds, like a running scorecard; helps decide if remedial action is necessary, such as rebuttal witnesses.

Voir Dire/Jury Selection

Chart to make notes

Opening Statement

Attorney notes

Stipulations and Pretrial Order

Copies of actual documents

Relevant Pleadings

The last amended pleading of each party; called "live" pleadings

Witnesses

Your witnesses in the order they are to be called
Include addresses and all phone numbers
Short characterization of relation to the case and what is to be
proved with each witness

Outline of questioning areas

Discovery

List of everything in this section

Your interrogatory answers, admissions, and documents
produced

Opponent's interrogatory answers, admissions, and documents
produced

Deposition summaries, highlighted for easy reference

Documents and Exhibits

List of everything in this section

If to be authenticated by a witness, put a copy with that witness's section in the notebook

References to audiovisual aids, blowups, charts

Briefing and Research

Trial briefs that are concise and succinct, ready to give to the judge, with copies for all counsel

Closing Argument

Attorney notes

Motions, Requests for Instructions, Jury Questions

Motion in limine
Pending motions yet to be ruled on

Requested jury instructions and questions

Finally, I'd like to say that as you work in different areas of litigation, you will need many forms. When you use a new one, add it to your personal form files. They will save you and your attorney much time. But remember to throw out old forms as you improve them, or as changes in the rules or the law make them obsolete.

Here are just a few more forms you might need at some point in a lawsuit.

Form: Medical Authorization

To Whom It May Concern:

This will authorize you to furnish to my attorneys, [name], any information they request concerning injuries to me [or child's name], including history, condition, diagnosis, treatment, and prognosis.

Do not furnish information or give medical reports to anyone other than my designated attorneys unless specifically authorized in writing by me.

[Signature and date]

Form: Confidentiality Agreement

For the consideration of Ten Dollars ($10) and other good and valuable consideration, the undersigned agrees to keep confidential the financial or other information pertaining to XYZ Corporation [or the terms of the settlement agreement, or whatever is being kept confidential].

XYZ Corporation agrees that the information may be given to the undersigned's designated attorney or accountant but that this agreement also applies to attorneys and accountants as to third parties.

When the case is all settled, you will need a settlement agreement. Usually it's prepared by the one paying the money, usually the defendant. Here is a plain language form that has just about every provision you might need, including a confidentiality provision. Use the paragraphs you need for your particular case. This form contains some legalese, just in case you are having withdrawal symptoms. But now that you are expert at making a document concise, chop away (especially on paragraph 3)!

Form: Settlement and Release Agreement

1. Settlement Payment: XXX and its attorneys acknowledge receipt of payment by YYY of $XXX.

2. Confidentiality: XXX and its attorneys agree that the terms of this agreement are confidential and that these terms and the amount of money paid to XXX or its attorneys have not been disclosed and will not be disclosed to any other person, except the following: the tax analysts or consultants who prepare the tax returns for XXX and their attorneys; the Internal Revenue Service; and any other person to whom disclosure is required by law or court order. Any person to whom disclosure is made will be instructed that the information is confidential and that the released parties' remedy for a willful or knowing breach of this confidentiality provision will be a suit for enforcement of all legal remedies available to the released parties.

3. Releases:

   A. In consideration of YYY's signing and delivery of this agreement and in consideration of the payment described in paragraph 1 above, XXX releases and forever discharges YYY and its officers, directors, shareholders, employees, agents, servants, predecessors, successors, insurance carriers, attorneys, and representatives, from all judgments, claims, disputes, demands, damages, debts, liabilities, obligations, contracts, agreements, causes of action, suits, and costs, whether in contract or in tort, known or unknown, anticipated or unanticipated, which XXX has or may have or claim to have against YYY by reason of any matter or omission alleged in [case number].

   B. XXX represents that it is the only entity having any interest in the matters released and that none of such claims, disputes, demands, damages, debts, liabilities, obligations, contracts, agreements, causes of action, suits, judgment, or costs, or any part, have been assigned, granted, or transferred in any way to any other person or entity, and that no other person or entity retains any right, title, or interest by subrogation or otherwise, other than in connection with XXX's employment of its attorneys.

C. XXX agrees to indemnify and hold harmless YYY from all claims, demands, liens, or causes of action, and the reasonable costs, including attorney's fees, incurred in defense of any third-party claim against XXX.

D. YYY releases XXX and its officers, directors, shareholders, employees, agents, servants, predecessors, successors, insurance carriers, attorneys, and representatives, from all judgments, claims, disputes, demands, damages, debts, liabilities, obligations, contracts, agreements, causes of action, suits, and costs, whether in contract or in tort, known or unknown, anticipated or unanticipated, which XXX has or may have or claim to have against YYY by reason of any matter or omission alleged in [case number].

4. Delivery of Documents: The parties and their attorneys will sign and deliver all documents and perform all further acts reasonably necessary to fulfill the provisions of this Agreement, including signing a motion to set aside XXX's judgment against YYY and dismiss YYY's appeal as to XXX, and any other documents necessary to set aside XXX's judgment against YYY in [case number].

5. Attorney's Fees, Expenses, and Costs. The parties agree that each will bear its own attorney's fees, expenses, and costs of suit incurred in [case number].

6. Joint Preparation of this Agreement. The parties participated jointly in the preparation of this agreement. Each party has had the opportunity to review, comment upon, and redraft this agreement. No rule of construction will apply against or in favor of any party.

7. No Admission of Liability or Wrongdoing. No party admits, stipulates, or concedes any liability or act of wrongdoing in connection with the matters alleged in [case number].

8. Parties Represented by Counsel. The parties have been represented by counsel of their own choice in the negotiations leading to this agreement, have read this agreement, and have had it fully explained by their counsel.

9. No Reliance on Representations. XXX agrees that it does not rely
    on, and has not relied on, any representation made by YYY other
    than those contained in this agreement.

10. Entire Agreement. This agreement embodies the entire agreement
    and understanding of the parties and supersedes all prior representa-
    tions, agreements, and understandings, oral or written. This agree-
    ment may be amended or terminated only in writing signed by XXX
    and YYY.

11. Controlling Law. This agreement is controlled by the laws of the
    state of Texas.

12. Successors and Assigns. This agreement is binding on the successors
    and assigns of the parties.

13. Authority of Signers. Each party represents and warrants that the
    person signing below is fully empowered and authorized to sign this
    agreement and to bind the person or entity shown below to the terms
    of this agreement.

SIGNED by the parties on [date] signifying acceptance.

[SIGNATURE BLOCKS]

*Finally, at some point in the lawsuit, your client may need a
power of attorney. Here is a form I edited down from six pages.
(I'm sure it can use some more cutting, and you should try it.)*

Form: General Durable Power of Attorney

STATE OF TEXAS   :
                          :
COUNTY OF HARRIS   :

    1. I, **CAROL ANN WILSON**, a resident of Houston, Harris
County, Texas, appoint my son, **DEVON KIRK**, of St. Louis,
Missouri, to serve as my attorney in my name and stead to do any act

and exercise any power that I myself can do, and I vest in my attorney full and general power of attorney, with authority to do for me any act or thing I could do personally.

2. This power of attorney will not terminate on my disability or incompetence but will be fully effective.

3. I ratify all acts done by my attorney under this general power of attorney and request that all persons give full effect to its terms, giving my attorney full power to act for me in any matter in which I might act if personally present.

4. Without limiting this general power of attorney, I wish to illustrate some of the powers granted in this document, so that third parties will accommodate my attorney's actions and requests:

    a. Open and close accounts, make deposits and withdrawals from any financial institution

    b. Buy, sell, transfer, assign, receive dividends from, renew, or cancel, any securities

    c. Buy, sell, transfer, mortgage, assign, manage, and supervise any real property

    d. Manage and negotiate any accounts with third parties

    e. Make and manage any investments and borrowings

    f. Transact all business with any government entity, including preparation, signing, and filing of any tax returns

    g. Transact all business with third parties for my health, support, and maintenance, whether medical or insurance-related

    h. Pursue or defend any lawsuits involving me

    i. Enter into, terminate, or amend any contracts involving me

j. Sign my name to any document requiring my signature, whether under oath or not

5. My attorney is not obligated to furnish any bond or security, and is to be reasonably compensated for his services, as he requests.

6. My attorney is authorized to appoint a substitute attorney for any period during which my attorney is unable to act for any reason.

7. Third parties are to deal with my attorney in good faith as though he were the unconditional owner and will incur no liability to me or to my heirs resulting from permitting my attorney to exercise any power, and my attorney is authorized to indemnify and hold harmless any third party who accepts my attorney's authority to act under this power.

8. This power of attorney may be revoked only in writing by me, notarized, to be effective on recording in the appropriate court records of the county of my residence.

9. The enumeration of the powers in paragraph 4 above does not limit or restrict the general powers granted to my attorney.

10. This instrument is signed and delivered in the state of Texas and Texas law will govern its validity and construction.

SIGNED on [date].

_____
Carol Ann Wilson

Signed and acknowledged before me by Carol Ann Wilson on [date].

_____
Notary Public, State of Texas

_____
Printed name of notary

My commission expires:

Bibliography

Albrecht, Steve, *The Paralegal's Desk Reference* (New York, Prentice Hall Inc., 1993)

The Bluebook, A Uniform System of Citation (15th ed.) (Cambridge, The Harvard Law Review Association, 1991)

Brohaugh, William, *Write Tight* (Cincinnati, Writer's Digest Books, 1993)

The Canadian Bar Association and The Canadian Bankers' Association, *The Decline and Fall of Gobbledygook: Reprt on Plain Language Documentation*, 1990

The Chicago Manual of Style (14th ed.) and *The Chicago Manual of Legal Style* (Chicago, University of Chicago Press, 1993)

Editors of Writer's Digest, *The Writer's Digest Guide to Good Writing*, (Cincinnati, Writer's Digest Books, 1994)

Elliott, David C., "A Model Plain-Language Act," *Texas Bar Journal*, December 1993, Volume 56

Esperti, Robert A. and Peterson, Renno L., *Loving Trust* (New York, Penguin Books 1991)

Flesch, Rudolf, *How to Write, Speak and Think More Effectively—Your Complete Course in the Art of Communication* (New York, Printer's Ink Publishing Corp., 1951, compilation by Signet Books, div. of Harper Collins Publishers, Inc., 1946)

Garner, Bryan A.
    A Dictionary of Modern Legal Usage (New York, Oxford University Press, Inc., 1987)
    The Elements of Legal Style (New York, Oxford University Press, Inc., 1991)

Hathaway, George, "Plain English—Ten-Year-Anniversary Theme Issue," *Michigan Bar Journal*, January 1994

Kimble, Joseph, *Plain English: A Charter for Clear Writing*, 9 Thomas M. Cooley L. Rev. 1 (1992)

Larbalestrier, Deborah E., *Paralegal Practice and Procedure* (Englewood Cliffs, Prentice Hall, Inc., 2d ed. 1986)

McCord, James W. H., *The Litigation Paralegal, A Systems Approach* (St. Paul, West Publishing Company, 2d ed. 1992)

McCormack, Mark H., *The Terrible Truth About Lawyers*, Mark H. McCormack Enterprises, Inc. 1987, Beech Tree Books, William Morrow & Co., New York; reprinted by Avon Books, a division of The Hearst Corporation, New York 1988, subtitled *What I Should Have Learned at Yale Law School*

Mellinkoff, David
    The Language of the Law (Boston, Brown Little & Co. 1963; 11th printing, 1990
    Legal Writing: Sense and Nonsense (St. Paul, West Publishing Company, 1982)

Mellinkoff's Dictionary of American Legal Usage (St. Paul, West Publishing Company, 1992)
"Plain English in the Law," *Michigan Bar Journal*, January 1994

National Association of Legal Secretaries, *Manual for the Lawyer's Assistant* (St. Paul, West Publishing Company, 3d ed., 1994)

Nelson, Noelle C., *A Winning Case* (Englewood Cliffs, Prentice Hall, Inc., 1991)

Sabin, William A., *The Gregg Reference Manual*, 7th ed. (New York, Macmillan-McGraw Hill, Glencoe Division, 1993)

Squires, Lynn B. and Rombauer, Marjorie Dick, *Legal Writing in a Nutshell* (St. Paul, West Publishing Company, 1982)

Statsky, William P. and Wernet, R. John Jr., *Case Analysis and Fundamentals of Legal Writing* (St. Paul, West Publishing Company, 1984)

Strunk, William Jr. and White, E.B., *The Elements of Style*, 3d ed. (New York, Macmillan Publishing Co., 1979)

Vanolia, Jan, *Wright Right!* (Berkely, Ten Speed Press, 1988)

APPENDIX A

A Skit for Your Use

If you want to have some fun with plain language, you have my permission to use this skit. I wrote it for a "Night in Court" program of the Greater Houston Legal Secretaries Association that featured Judge Lynn Hughes as guest speaker. This skit was a warmup for his talk.

You may use it in your professional associations or for your in-house CLE. You may use it as it appears here, amend it, or just enjoy reading it. I call it "The Legalese Disease."

"The Legalese Disease"
By
Carol Wilson, PLS, CLAS

Cast of Characters:

Judy: A brand-new legal secretary on her first job out of the local legal secretarial program

Maureen: A seasoned veteran of 20 years' experience, who has worked her way to secretary for the semiretired senior partner

Wordy: Third-year associate bucking for partnership

Scene: Two-secretary bay at a large law firm

 Judy: One HUGE earring; pencil behind her ear; glasses on top of her head; dictation earphones around her neck; legal dictionary

 Maureen: Polishing her nails

JUDY: Oh, Mr. Wordy will be in bright and early this morning wanting the final draft of this pleading, and I haven't been able to find all these words he used in any dictionary. (Looking through dictionary.) Hmmm, let's see.

     (To Maureen):   Do you know what "omnia praesumuntur contra spoliatorem" means?

MAUREEN: (Very dignified and haughty):   My dear, you cannot question what a lawyer writes. It's not our duty to know the meaning—only how to spell and type it.

JUDY: Oh, okay. But if I knew what it meant, it seems like there would be a better word for it.   This legal dictionary says "all things are presumed against a spoliator." I don't know what a "spoliator" is, and it's not in this dictionary, but "spoliation" is here and it says "the mutilation, or destruction, of something, e.g., the erasure or alteration of a writing." So I guess a spoliator would be something like a forger. Do you think that's right?

MAUREEN: Well, I'll see if I can find anything on it as soon as my nails dry. Did you look at Ballentine's?

JUDY: I don't know what that IS. It sounds like some kind of beer.

MAUREEN: It's a legal dictionary. We have one on a stand in the library three floors down, and it's three feet thick.

JUDY: Oh, well, I know it's spelled right, but I don't know why he didn't just say "forger."

MAUREEN: Well, it's probably one of those legal doctrines. If they say it in English, it doesn't sound legal.

JUDY: Well, even if it sounds legal, don't people have to understand it without going to the library to look it up?

You know, I don't even know why interest rates are quoted "per annum." Why don't they just say PER YEAR?

MAUREEN: (Answers phone): Mr. Bigwig's office, may I help you? (Pause.) Oh yes, he decided on the blue diamond, since this is their 50th anniversary. Can you have that ready by 2:30? (Pause.) Yes, the caterers will be there by noon, and they are going to decorate a special spot for the present. (Pause.) Oh, yes, it will be a nice party. They have invited about 500 of their closest and dearest friends. I've been working on it for weeks. I'll send one of our courthouse runners to pick it up. Thank you so very much.

JUDY: Oh, here's another one: "non culpabilis." It says it means "not guilty." Why didn't he just say "not guilty"?

And "fructus civiles"—all revenues, which, though not strictly fruits, are recognized as such by law, e.g., rent, interest, or profit.

This drives me crazy! (TURN PAGE QUICKLY.)

Oh, my GOD! Listen to this: "Voluntas in delictis, no exitus spectatur" That sounds like delicious volunteers can't get out if they're spectators. (Pause.) Wouldn't that be false imprisonment? The book says, "in crimes the intention, and not the consequence, is looked to." I guess that's another one of those legal doctrines. Do you think so?

MAUREEN: Beats me.

JUDY: And look at these: What's the difference between misfeasance, malfeasance, and nonfeasance? Have you ever heard of anybody feasancing? (Deliberately): I thought it was a *bird* that you Hunt, Kill, Cook, and Eat.

(Now hamming it up): Oh, here's a *great* one: "mater familias," the mother of the family. I'm *sure* the next time I call home, I'll ask to speak to "Mater Familias."

(Now giggling): And here's a John Lennon song: "Jus imaginis." Says it's from the Romans, meaning "the right of using statutes of ancestors."   (TURN QUICKLY.)

And *surely* I'll find a place to use this one at my next cocktail party: "furiosi nulla voluntas est." Now we have *furious* volunteers!   But it says it means "a madman has no free will, i.e., he is not criminally responsible." Well, one word will do it: *insane*—just like this pleading I'm trying to decipher!

MAUREEN: Is that a complaint you're working on?

JUDY: Yes, and it's in federal court, and so far, it's 47 pages, not including the exhibits. Mr. Wordy said it has to be filed today. My spell check is going haywire! I don't know if I'm gonna get it ready or not.

MAUREEN: Well, I sure hope it doesn't get assigned to Judge Hughes's court.

JUDY: Why?

MAUREEN: Oh, haven't you heard about him? He's been in the paper and everything. I saw an article the other day where a lawyer presented him an order to sign, and it had all the regular stuff about "on this blank day of blank, came on to be considered such and such and the court having considered, et cetera, is of the opinon that such motion should be and the same is hereby granted. It is therefore ordered, et cetera, et cetera." You know, all the standard stuff we have on all our forms going back to before the American Revolution.

And Judge Hughes took his pencil and marked all of it out and told the lawyer to redraft it. He redrafted it and Judge Hughes crossed it out again and told the lawyer he wasn't going to sign it until it he got it right. By the time he got through with it, it said "Plaintiffs are granted leave to file an amended complaint"—period!

JUDY: (In disbelief): REALLY???????

MAUREEN: Yes, and he has a whole list of things that are not allowed in pleadings in his court, and you wouldn't *believe* what's on that list: stuff we have in everything we do, like "Wherefore Premises Considered." How many times have you seen that, just in the short time you've been a legal secretary?

JUDY: Oh, that's on *everything*. I even have a macro for it, I use it so much.

MAUREEN: He also doesn't want "said" used as an article. You know, like "said automobile," or "said documents." I don't think lawyers can write without using that. I've never seen one that could.

And you can't use "and/or." Thank goodness somebody's standing up about that silly phrase. I don't think lawyers can write without using it. Don't you just *hate* it?

JUDY: Yes I do, and I never see it anywhere except in lawyers' writing.

MAUREEN: I heard Judge Hughes even *struck* a lawyer's entire pleading because he couldn't understand what it said. Threw it out. Gone. Zippo.

You know, the Federal Rules of Civil Procedure say "Pleadings shall be concise."

JUDY: AMEN, SISTER! (Back to her book): Oh, here is the greatest one. This one must be about Judge Hughes. "Rex non potest peccare." "The KING can do no wrong."

WORDY: (Rushing in, out of breath; drops entire file as he reaches Judy): Judy, Judy, Judy! I'm late! Is it ready????

JUDY: Yes, sir, it sure is, Mr. Wordy. I have *two* versions—yours, weighing in at 18 pounds—I just put it on the postage scale and *broke* it—and mine, which says "You forged it. We lost money because of it. And we want you to pay us."

The End

APPENDIX B

Editing Checklist

When editing an already created work, whether your boss's or your own, here are some fundamentals you may use as a checklist.

1. Is It Well Organized?

Are the important points up front?
Are there useful subheadings?
Does it have a logical beginning, middle, and end?
Have you said only what's necessary?

2. Is It Written FOR the Reader?

Does the document flow, and can the reader easily understand it?
Do you have to stop and reread any passages? If so, rework it.
Does it have short sentences?
Are there adequate pararaph breaks?
Have you eliminated unnecessary jargon?

3. Does It Look Good?

Have you reserved underlining, bolding, and italics for emphasis, or
is there too much, making it distracting?

Do you have nice margins and ample, eye-easing white space on the
pages, or does it all run together with no breaks?

4. Have You Eliminated the Useless Words?

Use the active voice instead of the passive voice.
     ("I hit the ball." rather than "The ball was hit.")

Use action verbs; don't rely on adverbs.

No tautologies or redundancies, like:
     "save and except"
     "release and acquit"
     "past history"
     "reason why"

No verbosity, like:
     "point in time"
     "in the event that"
     "reach a decision"
     "with reference to"
     "for the reason that"

INDEX

217